Live it Up!

Mark E. Petersen
of the Council of the Twelve

Published by DESERET BOOK COMPANY Salt Lake City, Utah 1971

Copyright 1971
by
DESERET BOOK COMPANY
ISBN 87747-450-8
Library of Congress No. 70-175717

Printed by

in the United States of America

Excerpts from an article in the July 1957
issue of Better Homes and Gardens Magazine copyrighted
and used by permission.

Table of Contents

Chapter	Title	Page
1	It's a Date!	1
2	The Dating Trend	5
3	What the Lord Thinks	11
4	Living it Up—or Down?	15
5	Muddled Standards	17
6	Filthy Films	23
7	What Promiscuity Costs	27
8	The Purpose of Dating	31
9	Eternal Standards	35
10	Born Free	41
11	The Sanctity of Sex	47
12	No Trial Marriages	51
13	Whom Shall We Date?	57
14	Short Skirts—Long Hair	61
15	Like Men or Like Women?	69
16	The Generation Gap	73
17	A New Significance	81
18	The Devil Is a Liar!	85
19	Today's World	89
20	Does It Help or Hurt?	93
21	What the "Big Ones" Say	97
22	You Only Live Once	103

It's a Date!

Chapter One

Susan was seventeen—and pretty. She had grown up with the usual teachings in the usual home. She was having a delightful time at school and the other kids liked her. In her senior year at Hoover High she met Burt, who was a fullback on the football team. He was a typical fullback—six feet tall, weighed 190 pounds, and was fast on his feet; handsome too! He had had an eye on Sue for weeks, but football practice crowded out his customary social life. Now the season was over. Christmas was approaching, and there was that last big dance before the holidays.

Meeting Susan in the hall one day he stopped her with, "Hi, beautiful." Flattered, she smiled and walked on, but he was soon at her side.

"Hi, Sue," he said, as he walked along with her. "What's doing?" Sue's heart beat jumped to well above normal in a hurry. Burt was one of the idols at the school. In every game that season he had scored at least one touchdown. Now to have him at her side—and to have the other kids see him there—was exciting to say the least.

"Hi, Burt," was her muffled reply. Her face flushed, making her more radiant than ever.

"How about the Christmas dance, Sue? Would you like to go?", he asked.

"Well, I really would," she said, almost in a whisper, hardly breathing by this time. It was a date.

At the dance they had a great time, but afterward———. How far should you go on a date? This was the question Sue had to face. Burt was aggressive. That's why he was so good on the football field. He now became aggressive with her. She found herself in a panic. As he made advances, and she held him back, her brain worked like lightning. All the things her mother and father had taught her about dating now flashed through her mind. She thought of the bishop of the ward and of her Laurel leader, and the other girls in M.I.A.

Suddenly she realized that she faced a grave decision. Right here, on this date with Burt, she found herself at a most important crossroad in her life. Here and now she could go either of two ways, and each one would be significant. Her mind flashed into the future too, working like a computer. What did she want in life? Could this date with Burt help her or hurt her in reaching her long-cherished aims? How far should she let him go with her?

Lightning-quick thoughts now reminded her that Burt had never shown any interest in her before, and that now on this first date his main and only apparent interest was not in her at all, that is, not in her real self. Obviously, all he wanted was a pretty face and a comely form in a situation that had nothing to recommend it.

She suddenly remembered what she had read in a book on dating written by the late Prof. Frank W. Hoffer of the University of Virginia. She had been so impressed by his words that she had memorized them:

"When a boy who has no sincere feeling toward a girl tempts her to neck or pet, he is simply offering her a price tag of cheapness to hang around her neck, for that is his evaluation of her. If she accepts and wears the price tag, that is her evaluation of herself."

That flash of memory was all it took, and Sue instantly walked out on Burt. She went home a sadder and a wiser, but also a very grateful girl.

"Thank heaven," she said to herself, "for the teachings of sane adults."

The Dating Trend

Chapter Two

Burt had promised Sue a good time. While they were out together he had constantly talked about "living it up." He knew that she was a conservative type, and took it upon himself to "turn her on."

"All the kids are doing it," he had told her, and yet he had no real interest in her. She was pretty and she was comely, she had a disarming smile and her eyes seemed full of fun, but she was what the boys had come to regard as being on the slow side.

Burt was interested in girls merely as objects of fun. At his age, of course, he had no serious intentions towards any of them. To him they were just toys to be played with for an evening, and then dropped and forgotten when the next pretty face came along. And what about the stain he left behind? About that he couldn't care less! Unfortunately, Burt wasn't so different.

A tendency toward petting or worse has been growing among young people for a number of years, and is reaching a peak just now. It was encouraged by the moral breakdown which occurred in the second World War, and afterward. Each year it has become a little worse.

As far back as 1957, the noted writer Howard Whitman, describing conditions which existed then, in an article in "Better Homes and Gardens," said this:

"A poll among male students of a midwestern university indicated their dating expectations as follows:

"Seventy-nine per cent expected a girl to neck with him by the time he had had three dates with her; 52 per cent expected her also to pet within the same period.

"It didn't matter to them who the girl was, or how deeply they felt about her (if they had feelings at all).

"It is doubtful whether in the era of the moral muddle the students recognized this as a sheer USE of one person by another. The age of liberation has failed to note this form of aggression, failed to distinguish between the freedom of any individual to maintain a right to privacy, and the 'freedom' to exploit another person for momentary, personal physical satisfaction."*

Mr. Whitman's poll was taken in 1957, and conditions may have changed in the areas he contacted. But more recent polls by other experts indicate that the condition has become worse instead of better, and is a strong warning to all right minded persons.

Petting is evil, whether on the first date or the hundredth. It is a partial loss of virtue and may quickly and almost unexpectedly lead to a complete loss of that most priceless possession. The fact that it is common among young people of the world—and it is dreadfully common—is no argument in its favor. When it is spoken of as "just a little lovin' " the facts in the case are not changed. It is one of the traps of the "new morality cult" which recognizes no moral standards at all.

No amount of personal acquaintanceship, no number of promises to "go steady," no ridicule of the "old-fashioned standards", however severe, can justify

---

*Copyright Meredith Corp. 1957. All rights reserved. Used by permission.

petting in the least. It is lustful, sensual and degrading. It robs boys and girls alike of self-respect and respect for each other. Any boy who expects to take advantage of a girl by the third date, or on any date, has only a lustful purpose in mind. Girls should realize that their bodies are sacred, not to be profaned by predatory boys who are hungry for physical excitement. Our bodies are God-given. They are temples of the Holy Spirit, and are not to be turned over to Satan and his followers for lustful purposes.

The world may neck and pet, but Latter-day Saints must be different—so different that we will not partake of the sins of "Babylon", that we may not in turn suffer from her plagues, as the scripture has expressed it.

We are to be a peculiar people, as the Apostle Peter said, peculiar in being clean when the world is unclean, faithful when the world denies faith.

As God's people, we most certainly must not be OF the world, even though we live in it. The whole basic concept of our religion rests on the principle that we shall be different from the world because we are his people and must be clean and faithful.

Latter-day Saint boys are holders of the holy priesthood. They administer the Sacrament of the Lord's Supper. They go on missions. As young elders they bless the sick. As priests they perform baptisms, and why? That humble, repentant souls may receive a remission of their sins and enter the Church by that sacred ordinance.

Can sinful priests please the Lord by officiating at the baptismal font where remission of sins is granted to repentant people? Can sinful Aaronic Priesthood holders minister at the sacrament table without displeasing their Heavenly Father?

The sacrament is probably our most sacred ordinance. Should stained hands touch its emblems? Should a voice used for seductive purposes offer the prayer?

Let us be realistic about this important aspect of our religious lives, and remember that the Lord has commanded: "Be ye clean that bear the vessels of the Lord."

Girls are not toys and neither are they "fair game" for any boy. Dates among Latter-day Saint young people must never be for seductive purposes. They must offer an opportunity in decency for young people to associate together in trust and confidence.

No date is worth a loss of virtue, even a partial loss. No date can compensate for the despair that comes through yielding to temptation. Girls are better off without dates of any kind than to subject themselves to the wicked enticements of evil boys who regard them as mere playthings.

"But who wants to be left out of the crowd?" is the cry of those who are willing to accept such advances as the price of an evening out. The logical answer, of course, is "no one." And none need be left out.

We are a Church of three million members, with half the Church population under 25 years of age. We are a young people's Church. With such a tremendous population of young people, there is no reason why Latter-day Saint youth in most areas cannot find ample wholesome companionship within their own circle, if they will but seek it.

Doesn't the Lord caution us against involvements with unbelievers? That was a theme with the Apostle Paul. We can form our own social groups. We have them within the structure of the Church. It is only for young people to USE those facilities and be blessed, and they will escape the alluring advancements of selfish people whose uncontrolled physical urges could spell disaster. We are the Zion of the Lord, and he has defined Zion as "the pure in heart."

Statistics such as those provided by Mr. Whitman should put every decent boy and girl on guard, reminding them that we cannot be like the world nor adopt her wicked ways, because we are the Lord's youth.

He has a great mission for us. Let us prepare for it.

Certainly no Latter-day Saint boy should ever lead a girl into a moral trap, and no girl should hesitate to walk, or even run out on a date—just as did Sue—under similar circumstances. In a situation of that kind, flight is the best answer. Better be safe than sorry.

What the Lord Thinks

Chapter Three

As Latter-day Saints we must be deeply concerned about good morals. Our religion places great emphasis upon them. But why? Why do we need to be so different from the rest of the world?

It is because we are to become like our Heavenly Father, and we can do so only if we will obey him. That is no idle thought. It is a reality.

We are the literal children of God. We are placed here to learn to become like him through testing and through trial.

Anybody can take the downward path. Anyone can drift with the current and the crowd. That requires neither effort nor brains! But the Lord expects us, his Zion of Latter Days, to rise above the world.

We must be beacons on the hill. Not only must we save ourselves in righteousness and purity, but by our examples we must help to save others.

Let us not suppose that "everybody does it" when we speak of the sins of the world. Everyone does not! There are still millions of good people in the world, and hosts of wholesome youth who have no sympathy with the lowered moral standards. That is why we send missionaries out to bring them into the Church.

The Positive Side

The vast majority of our people—regardless of race, creed, color, or economic status—are respectable, reasonable, responsible citizens. Last year, for example:

More than 196,000,000 of our people were *not* arrested.

More than 89,000,000 married persons did *not* file for divorce.

More than 115,000,000 individuals maintained a formal affiliation with some religious group.

More than 75,000,000 citizens and corporations paid more than $106,000,000,000 in income taxes.

More than 49,000,000 students did *not* riot or petition to destroy our system.

More than 4,000,000 teachers, preachers and professors did *not* strike or participate in riotous demonstrations.

More than 9,000,000 of our young men did *not* burn their draft cards.

Challenges of Our Times
by Charles L. Gould

We must not be misled into supposing that just because the noisy minority lowers their own standards, and tries to make sin look like glittering gold, that it is desirable.

Sin was always sin, and there is no happiness in it. On the other hand, the price of sin is dreadful, as we shall see in a later chapter.

As Latter-day Saints, and believers in the Lord should we not seek to find out what he thinks about morals? He condemns illicit sex relations as among the worst of all sins.

To his erring son, the Prophet Alma (Alma 39) taught the law of chastity with boldness and clarity, and told him how deep was the sin he had committed. Illicit sex sin, he said, is one of the three worst offenses in the category established by the Lord. The first is sin against the Holy Ghost, the second is murder, and the third is sex sin.

There is no forgiveness for the first two, but if we have committed sex sin in the past, and will fully repent, the Lord will forgive us. And yet if we become "repeaters," he has said (D&C 42) we will be cast out.

But as to petting, what does the Lord say? In the Sermon on the Mount he said: "Whosoever looketh upon a woman to lust after her hath committed adultery with her already in his heart."

Can any boy "pet" without lust? And if a girl permits a boy to so arouse her passions that she allows him to handle her body in a petting party, can she be without lust either? Or even worse, what if she returns the petting?

Is there anything "virtuous, lovely, or of good report, or praiseworthy" in a petting party?

When the Saviour gave the Sermon on the Mount to the Nephites he added this, as he taught complete chastity:

"Behold, I give you a commandment, that ye suffer none of these things to enter your heart. For it is better that ye should deny yourselves of these things, wherein ye will take up your cross, than that ye should be cast into hell."

Is not that too high a price to pay for such an experience?

The Savior is the Creator. He made us, and knows about all our natural feelings and human urges, and in the light of that knowledge he gave us this law. In modern revelation, he put it this way:

"He that looketh upon a woman to lust after her SHALL DENY THE FAITH AND SHALL NOT HAVE THE SPIRIT, and if he repents not he shall be cast out." (D&C 42:23)

And of course the same rule applies to both female and male. If we are to be true Latter-day Saints, and not make our religion a mockery, should we not be wholehearted about it, and believe the Christ and his teachings?

When he tells us to refrain from sex sin—even with our eyes—shall we not obey him? Who, with any regard for the Lord, would want to lose the Spirit or deny the faith, or be "cast into hell"?

Sex abuse is the devil's trap.

Living it Up— or Down?

Chapter Four

The cry today is to "live it up." With this we agree —if it is really UP!

Sadly, though, the expression as used now generally means what the world regards as a good time through indulgence, either in liquor, drugs, sex, or other deviations. It is downward living!

It puts us on a toboggan which most assuredly can give us our fill of excitement at every curve on the hill, but it takes us down, and down, and down.

Everyone knows there is more to life than fun, with its so-called "thrills," derived from physical satisfactions. There is also hardship and grief, suffering and disappointment, whereas there should be growth and character development.

No one can have only fun, not in this mortal sphere. Even on a toboggan, breath-taking as it is, there is always the bottom to contemplate as we race downward, not to mention the hazards of dangerous curves, rocks and trees on the coasting hill. And who can really shut their eyes to them, try as they may?

Fun by itself is just a bubble. The deeper emotion is the joy of growth and development, and it always comes from the good and the clean.

Fun—what does the dictionary say about it? Mr. Webster says fun is "sport, merriment; to joke; to befool." And of "befool" he says: "to delude or lead into error, to deceive, or to treat as a fool" (as Burt tried to treat Sue).

But the learned scholar defines *Joy* as "the emotion excited by the expectation of good; that which causes happiness." Of happiness he explains: "it is the state of well being or blessedness, a state of prosperity." And when he defines prosperity he calls it "the state or condition of successful progress."

Then what should we seek in life? "The state or condition of successful progress," progress toward becoming like our Father in Heaven, which is the exact purpose of life.

No one needs to fail. God did not send us here for that. He planned for our success and gave us the necessary guidelines to achieve it. But we ourselves must adhere to those guidelines, or we will derive no benefit from them.

No one else can make up our minds or our final decisions, and no one else can GROW for us, just as no one else can actually make us happy. Happiness is anchored to good character, and good character is of our own making.

In "living it up" then, we must avoid the downward course. If we are going to "live it up" we must make certain that it is really UP. It is the ladder and not the toboggan that must be our choice.

Muddled Standards
Chapter Five

A sixteen-year-old California girl walked into a doctor's office. She was visibly shaken and highly nervous. After the examination the doctor told her she was to become a mother.

"But I'm not married!" she gasped, and then she broke down in tears. Quieted somewhat after a long and kindly talk with the doctor, she dried her tears and said, "Well, really, doctor, I didn't think it was wrong any more. I thought things had changed."

So much has been said by the advocates of "liberation" that many of the youth have been misled into thinking that the "old-fashioned" standards really had changed and were no longer binding. In this day of "anything goes," virtue has been maligned and ridiculed in many circles. And with what results?

New highs in illegitimacy.

A crushing divorce burden.

A greatly increased psychiatric load.

A multiple increase in teenage suicides.

A 400 per cent increase in venereal disease among people from 14 to 19 years of age—and this in five years! But that isn't all. When Howard Whitman wrote his paper on "Youth and the Natural Urge," he included the following startling facts of that day:

"Girls are hurt more than boys in the era of moral confusion because upon them falls the crushing burden of pregnancy. Even forced marriage is not always the answer. Call these, if you will, the more fortunate ones. The less fortunate ones provide a steadily increasing business for abortion mills and a new and grisly racket which has sprung up in recent years—baby selling. It is estimated that 20,000 girls each year fall into the hands of baby racketeers.

"In return for confinement in a shabby room where they can give birth in secret, their babies are taken from them, given forged birth certificates, and sold in the illegal adoption market at $2,000 to $3,000 each. Evidence gathered by the U. S. Senate Subcommittee to Investigate Juvenile Delinquency points to coast-to-coast baby racketeering with profits of some $50,000,000 a year, a human merchandising operation as disgraceful as the slave trade.

"Ernest Mitler, special counsel to the sub-committee, said to me: 'We have seen cases where the girls are given papers to sign when they are not yet out of the anesthetic—signing away their babies. If they object later they are blackmailed with threats of publicity. Shame and the racket have them caught in the middle.'"

Drugs come into this picture too, becoming a frightful part of some dating habits. A nineteen-year-old girl came to the U.S. Public Health Service hospital in Lexington, Kentucky for help. She was a drug addict who had taken up the habit, she thought, quite innocently. She wanted so much to hold on to her boy friend, that she was willing to lower any bars to do so. And this she did.

"I started going with this fellow like all other girls did," she explained. "Sure, I had ideas about purity and all that. But you start reading things and seeing movies, and you begin to think you're old-fashioned. So I got involved......................"

She was 17 when she became "involved" with this older boy. He was already on narcotics. At 18 she took up drugs too. If they were good for him they would not hurt her, she rationalized, and anyway she wanted to hold on to her lover by doing whatever he did.

At 19 the police arrested her. She had entered prostitution to "earn" money to supply drugs for her boy friend and herself. Now she was "hooked."

Muddled youth? So many are. And why are they muddled? Very largely because the adults have made them so, for hosts of adults are as muddled as they. It began when many adults no longer wanted to live up to the old and true standards of conduct which had made our nation great, and which had been laid down as far back as Moses.

Our age became permissive, to use the popular word, which means "anything goes." And that in turn means the discard of restrictions which obstruct the "anything goes" philosophy. Remove restrictions and moral collapse follows just as waters flow when the dam is removed.

Immorality has been paraded under the guise of "a new morality," which for a time was endorsed by many legislators, educators, and even by some clergymen. New laws were passed protecting the immoral. Girls were allowed to enter prostitution at 16. Homosexual activity was given a legal status. Pre-marital sex was approved by some as a trial before marriage.

The Lord in ancient times made adultery a capital crime. Fornication came under a similar rule. Men and women who engaged in homosexual activity were executed on the spot. It was all an abomination in his sight.

But today? Many tell themselves there is no God, and therefore his supposed laws are not binding. They say the Bible is a myth and therefore we need pay no more heed to it.

Pornographic publications multiply, and their filth invades even responsible magazines, newspapers and TV stations. It all has but one aim—to destroy morals and give license to corruption.

When restrictions are removed from filth, many also try to remove the stigma which has been associated with sin for so long. They say that sex abuse is now legal; therefore, there is no wrong in it, so "let's go—the sky is the limit."

But is it really the sky, or are they confused in their directions as they head the opposite way? They forget that they cannot change God's laws by their own volition. Immorality has been popular before, but always it has ended like Sodom and Gomorrah, and it always will.

With the introduction of the "pill" and other contraceptives, some wayward youth feel that there is little danger of pregnancy any more, so this affords another opportunity to remove the "lid" of restraint.

How little they know of the dangerous "side-effects" of these new contraceptives, which doctors warn can bring death and severe illness.

As some adults have forced their wicked philosophies and practices upon the public, many of the youth followed suit, just as confused as they. And who will pay the price? The adults? Yes, by all means. But what of the erring youth? They will pay too for their own sins.

But is there no escape?

There is always an escape—for the repentant and obedient. We reap what we sow, and if we sow the seeds of cleanliness and virtue, and if we are truly repentant, we will receive the rewards of righteousness in happiness, successful living and prosperity. This is the group which really lives it UP.

When we see the whole picture of the corruption "conspiracy," and know what it is, we need not be enmeshed by it. Like a pilot on a ship, each one of us can steer away from the dangerous shoals about us, into the safe waters of chastity.

Filthy Films
Chapter Six

June and Clark went to a movie. June had serious reservations about the particular film they were to see. She had heard the other girls discussing it and knew it to be an obscene one. It was rated "X" by the industry itself.

Clark wanted to see it, and insisted that she accompany him and "stop being a prude." She told him frankly what she thought of the picture, but he argued that it wasn't that way at all; it was an "award" picture, and if it was as bad as June had heard, it would never have been granted the award. All of this was assumption on his part, and little of it was true.

June had wanted a date with Clark, but not to a movie of this kind. At last, under his constant coaxing, she agreed to go. The film portrayed a typical girl of the street with her loves and lovers. It was carnal and sensual, just as the other girls had told her. When telling June what kind of a picture it was, they all had said, "Look out for your date—he may get emotional." But to keep her friendship with Clark she decided to risk it.

Had June followed her best inclinations, as the picture got under way, she would have walked out on it at once, and did suggest doing so to Clark. But he refused. He had paid to see the picture and he was going to see it.

As they watched the suggestive scenes on the screen she noticed Clark begin to move closer and put his arms around her. Soon his hands began to wander. That June would not allow.

Frightened by the way the film affected Clark, she knew that she was in for some trouble unless she acted at once. Without saying another word, for she had already remonstrated with Clark, she jumped from her seat and literally ran for the exit. Hurrying on still further, she made her way to the nearest taxi stand, hired a cab and went home.

Clark at first started to follow her, but got no farther than the aisle when he turned back. He wanted to see that picture with or without June. But June had learned her lesson, and vowed never to see either Clark or a film like that again. If he wanted that sort of thing he was welcome to it, but not with her.

Suggestive movies have led thousands of young people into sex traps. Hot love-making on the screen has become a pattern for similar conduct on a date for many young people. This kind of love-making is in no way related to affection. It is exploitation of the girl by the boy, and it costs the girl the most.

Other forms of pornography are in the same class, whether they be magazines, newspapers, photographs, devices which come through the mail, or even TV performances. Every form of pornography appeals to the baser nature.

They all promote destruction of morals and good character. Each one opens the way for boys to USE girls as though they were property, mere sex objects, playthings for evil-minded men who respect neither the girls nor themselves.

Can Latter-day Saints, who are seeking to live the gospel, honor their priesthood, and develop into well-balanced men and women allow such a degradation of themselves as pornography portrays?

Once again Latter-day Saint youth must make a decision. Will they go the way of the Lord, or the way of evil? Once again we are persuaded to ask, "Who's on the Lord's side, Who?" And we remind ourselves:

> "Now is the time to show.
> We ask it fearlessly,
> Who's on the Lord's side, who?"

What Promiscuity Costs

Chapter Seven

Without laboring this unpleasant subject, we should at least know the costs of promiscuous sex indulgence. Not only does it violate the laws of God and degrade each person who indulges, but it is now spreading venereal disease in the world at a rate which causes some of the public health officials to label it an epidemic. One doctor has said that it has exceeded the epidemic stage—it is now a plague.

Nearly two thousand teenagers become infected with these diseases every day in the United States. Most of them receive no medical treatment. Of those who receive no treatment for syphilis:

> One in fifteen develops heart trouble.
> One in 25 becomes a cripple.
> One in 50 goes insane.
> One in 200 goes blind.

A thousand Americans die every month from syphilis. It has become one of our major killers. No one knows how many cases of venereal disease there really are, for usually they are kept hidden, and nearly always go without treatment, so that doctors are not able to make accurate reports required by law.

Dr. Walter H. Smartt, chief of the division of Venereal Disease Control in the Los Angeles, California County Health Department, told a medical convention in Salt Lake City that new cases of syphilis were up 54 per cent in Los Angeles County alone, in spite of the expenditure of a million dollars a year to combat the disease. He said further that there are fifty times more cases of gonorrhea than there are of syphilis.

In Los Angeles County 20 per cent of all high school graduates are infected, he said, adding that 10 per cent of all people in that area between the ages of 14 and 25 have the disease. Consider that staggering statement. Walk down the street there; count one in every ten persons you meet. If those persons are between the ages of 14 and 25, one in every ten you meet is infected with this disease.

The United States government spends over $70,000,000 a year to care for the unfortunate victims of the disease—those who become blind, crippled, or insane, or who develop syphilitic heart trouble. Another $40,000,000 a year is spent to combat the disease.

Although the problem is so widespread in Los Angeles County, it is equally, or more so in many other communities. The greatest incidence of the two diseases is in the area of Chicago, but all large cities are severely afflicted by it, and rural areas are beginning to feel the plague.

Untreated youngsters who become promiscuous pass it on freely to others with whom they associate. They in turn become carriers also, and thus it spreads. Among the worst carriers of the disease are the homosexuals. There are about 20,000,000 homosexuals in the United States. Not all have the disease, but many thousands do.

And what about treatment? Some forms of the disease can be wiped out by penicillin. But THE BAC-

TERIA CAUSING THIS PLAGUE ARE BECOMING RESISTANT TO ANTI-BIOTICS. The strain of gonorrhea being brought back into the states by many servicemen who have served with the military in Vietnam is penicillin-resistant, making the problem even more complex.

There is no medical preventive for these diseases. No innoculation or vaccination has ever been devised which can protect the promiscuous against infection. Only chastity will prevent it. Can any sane person suppose that a few moments of sexual stimulation is worth this kind of risk?

But again there is the Lord's side of the question. He commands complete purity of mind and body. For "kicks" shall we turn our back upon him? For "kicks" shall we endanger those whom we love most? Shall we, just for "kicks," take steps which may cause our own offspring to be born blind, insane, or crippled? A helpless babe—with every right to be well-born—just for "kicks," shall we jeopardize his very life? Many syphilitic babies die because of the infection received from their mothers. Would they not have been more fortunate if they had died, instead of living in the awful state of physical corruption and devastation which this disease thrusts upon them, innocent as they are? And what right does any person have to impose this affliction on a helpless child?

The Purpose of Dating

Chapter Eight

It is natural to date. Every right-thinking young person has a native desire to become acquainted with the opposite sex, looking eventually to pairing off in honorable marriage. But what about steady dating? When should it begin? What will we do on a date? How far shall we go in personal attachments?

For some years now it has been a custom in many areas for young people to begin steady dating as early as 14 and 15 years of age, which is a serious mistake. It has been the advice of the Church that steady dating should be delayed until we are old enough and mature enough and well enough established economically to consider marriage. Steady dating in the early teens has been disastrous to youth in many ways. The moral question always raises its head in such a situation, and this familiarity leads to many other problems.

Said one boy of 17: "When you go steady there is just naturally the danger of going too far."

And a 15-year-old girl said: "It is hard to keep things under control, being together so much."

Howard Whitman, in his illuminating discussions on this subject, calls attention to an interesting experiment in Lynn, Massachusetts, where one high school principal prohibited steady dating among the students.

After visiting the school Mr. Whitman said: "I expected to find a great swell of discontent among the students, a disgruntled feeling that they were being gypped. But no such thing. The youngsters were glad to be free to circulate again."

He quoted one coed as saying: "Going steady got to be a trap. You had to do it just because everybody else did. And sometimes you wished you were free to date another boy, but you couldn't because you were tied to the same one."

One of the school's football players was quoted by Mr. Whitman as saying: "Going steady got to be a fad, and like most fads, kids went overboard. You'd go to a dance and never dance with anybody but the same girl. It's lots more fun now since the school prohibited it."

A girl student commented: "At the dances we can now broaden our acquaintance, and get to meet some of the other boys. Dates are more interesting too, and since it is not always the same boy, there's more to talk about."

Another girl, quoted by Mr. Whitman, said: "We don't think it's a badge of honor any more to have a steady boy friend. It's more like an admission of failure. Any girl can get one date. The trick is how to get several."

And comments Mr. Whitman:

> "The going-steady craze is waning in some communities as the youngsters themselves become bored by being with the same partner all the time, or stung by the heartbreak of being thrown over in favor of another 'steady' or just plain being unwilling to be somebody else's exclusive property.
>
> "And so the good old American custom of playing the field may be coming back into its own again. It is a healthier

custom. Adolescence is meant to be a period of learning about the opposite sex, making wider acquaintanceships, finding out about character—preparation of the eventual selection of a mate.

"These values are lost," he continued, "if young people go steady years before they can even consider marriage. Instead there are dangers of involvement in situations too difficult to handle."

Then this wise man continues, as he wrote for "Better Homes and Gardens" in his illuminating article, "Youth and the Natural Urge":

"The era of the muddled standard has given youth ambiguous road signs, detours, confused directions. Can we do better now? Let's face it: adolescents are physically mature—they are capable of having children; but they are neither psychologically nor socially mature. So there is a gap to fill.

"During this growing-up period what happens to the 'natural urge'? We can't simply suspend it. It is foolhardy to deny it. And we're asking for trouble when we drive it underground. Adolescents will go in for some kind of physical expression, starting with hand-holding and on to good-night kissing.

"This too is part of natural growth. It forms a bridge to the full physical relationship in marriage, just as getting to know another youngster's character forms a bridge to the psychological relationship.

"The question is: How far to go?

"It can only be answered by seeing the dating period in perspective as part of the panorama of life. Dating is a preparation for marriage, starting with high school dances and on up through serious courtship. But it cannot be a SUBSTITUTE for marriage, either in the physical aspect or any other. The bridge cannot also be the goal.

"Ideally a youngster would progress step by step through the dating years. First, attractions for many members of the opposite sex, to get to know them, to learn about varying personalities, to shape one's own ideals. Next, a narrowing down, and finally a deep and meaningful relationship towards the goal of oneness—and then to make the goal a reality."

Eternal Standards
Chapter Nine

God's standards cannot change. He is the same yesterday, today and forever, and his formula for success is as unchangeable as he is. Worldly practices can change, but not the eternal verities upon which our success both here and in eternity is based.

We must remember that we are eternal beings, and not mere mortals who are here for a few years and then to sink into oblivion. We are everlasting. We cannot die and never will. We are the eternal offspring of God, we are spirits, his children, and we can no more die than he can. Our bodies are only houses in which we live, but we are eternal spirit beings with an eternal destiny.

God's formulae in nature are as eternal as his formulae in morals and spirituality. Water, for example, is always water, and can be broken down only in terms of H_2O. No matter what chemical combinations we make, we never have water unless we follow the Lord's formula. No man devised that formula. Only the Creator could do that, and H_2O cannot and never will be anything else but water.

It is the same with simple table salt, with which we are all acquainted. There is only one formula for table salt we all use as a savory. It is NaCl, and nothing else.

One of the interesting things about our space explorations is that scientists have discovered that all of the planets have essentially the same elements as are found on this earth. There is a striking uniformity in all creation.

No matter how old this earth is, or how young other planets may be, the same elements are there. This is shown in spectroscopic studies very clearly. Astronomers have noted that there is a uniformity in all of the galaxies. The same natural laws are followed.

It is also true of the moon. As our astronauts bring back samples of rocks, what do they find? That those rocks are similar to those on this earth, and similar to what telescopic studies indicate are on other planets too. In nature, God's formulae are everlasting, as scientists who study the age of the moon all know.

Some people wonder if there are other planets in space which may be inhabited. Although such a thing was scoffed at a few years ago, now with the present space studies scholars are rapidly changing their minds.

For example, Dr. Harlow Shapley, in his "Of Stars and Men" (page 74), says that in his opinion there are at least a hundred million planets on which it is reasonable to suppose that life could or does exist under conditions similar to those on our earth. To which Dr. Henry Eyring, in his "The Faith of a Scientist," responds:

> "It is accordingly natural to conclude that the universe is flooded with intelligent beings and presumably always has been. Any unfolding of intelligences that may eventuate on this earth only repeats what has happened previously elsewhere."

What are these people like, these inhabitants of other worlds? They are God's offspring as we are ourselves! And how do we know? Because the Lord, by revelation, tells us so. Note this scripture:

> "We heard the voice bearing record that he (Jesus) is the Only Begotten of the Father—that by him and through him and of him, the worlds are and were created AND THE INHABITANTS THEREOF ARE BEGOTTEN SONS AND DAUGHTERS UNTO GOD." (D.&C. 76:23-24)

We also are the "offspring of God", as Paul taught (Acts 17) and therefore the inhabitants of these other planets are our brothers and sisters, since we are all the begotten sons and daughters of God.

God's formula must be the same for all of his children, no matter on which planet they may live, and that formula is: "Be ye therefore perfect, even as your Father which is in Heaven is perfect." (Matt. 5:48)

His gospel then is the formula for becoming perfect like he is. He is an eternal being. We are also. He is exalted. We can be, and if we are faithful we will become like him. Therefore, his gospel is the means of our becoming so.

Then can he alter his eternal plan to suit the desires of fickle men? Of course not. And this is the reason we are told to be faithful to the end—living according to the formula—because we must be consistent in our growth toward perfection.

His plan for our eternal development cannot be subject to change any more than the chemical formula for drinking water, or table salt, or hydrochloric acid.

But do not the changing times, fashions, economics and whims of men alter our way of life? Most assuredly, if we allow them to. But they do not change God's laws and standards any more than they could change the formula of H_2O. To them we must hold regardless of what others may do.

The Lord's law on morals is the same today as it was when Potiphar's wife in Egypt "cast her eyes upon Joseph and said, "Lie with me." He refused, and replied, "How can I do this great wickedness and sin against God?" (Genesis 39)

Neither has it changed since Alma told his son, Corianton, that in associating with Isabel the harlot he had committed a sin "most abominable above all sins, save it be the shedding of innocent blood or denying the Holy Ghost." (Alma 39)

But some will ask, Must we always live by the old standards? Why not change with the times and keep abreast of things? Aren't we becoming more enlightened all the time? Isn't the reservoir of knowledge today far beyond anything known to man in the day when God said to Moses: "Thou shalt not commit adultery"?

The reservoir of knowledge truly is increasing rapidly. It is said that the available knowledge doubles every seven years, so rapidly are new developments coming on. But this increase is in SCIENTIFIC fields, and not in moral or spiritual matters.

Human nature has not changed over the centuries, nor have the "ways of a man with a maid". The moral laws of God were given to help us direct our human nature in the proper way. Human nature, at some time, is to develop into divine nature, because the intent of our creation is to become like God.

There has always been a conflict between human nature and divine nature, for the reason that we are mortal and subject to sin. We were made so by the Lord that we might exercise our free agency and choose between good and evil, thus allowing us to develop our own characters without compulsion.

If, of our own free will, we choose evil ways, and thus become filthy and devilish, we have no one to blame but ourselves.

If, also of our own free will, we choose righteousness, we then develop good character and eventually can become like our Father in Heaven. But becoming like him requires that we follow a definite formula, an unchanging one, that will help us to become perfect as he is.

There certainly is no perfection in filth or moral deviation. Perfection comes only by following the formula. God is pure. To be like him, we also must be pure. To help us achieve this purity he gave us the moral law.

You say times change? They do. Men fly today, but they couldn't in Moses' day. Astronauts go to the moon these days, a thing regarded as impossible only a few years ago. But the astronauts and the airplane pilots are nevertheless men—only men—with the same emotions, nature, likes and dislikes, as the people in Moses' day. Human nature has never changed over the centuries. Any history book will show that.

We speak of the barbaric actions of centuries ago, and wonder how men could be so cruel. But could there be anything more barbaric than the tortures inflicted on prisoners of war by the North Vietnamese, or by American troops who shoot down innocent Oriental men, women and little babies?

The occult also is with us today in the same forms known in the days of Saul and the witch of Endor. And we have the same kind of brothels used in ancient Egypt and Rome.

Drunkenness is at least as prevalent now as in the days of Ahab and Jezebel, and homosexuality exists now in the same form practiced in Gomorrha, ancient Egypt and Babylonia. It matters not whether we ride in oxcarts or airplanes, the method of transportation does not alter our characters, nor our natural urges, passions and emotions.

The man who plowed with a stick (and some still do this in underprivileged lands) is as much a child of God as the men who flew to the moon. He can become God-like in the same way too.

The facilities man possesses do not in any way alter his relationship to God. It is what is inside the man that counts—his heart, his desires, his passions. And every generation from Adam to the present has been the same in this respect.

All can become like God, but only in the same prescribed way. That is because he is unchangeable; that is why the gospel is eternal. It is the one and only formula for becoming like God, and as the gospel does not and cannot change, so its standards of conduct must be the same forever.

In the days of the Apostle Paul he taught this:

"Know ye not that the unrighteous shall not inherit the kingdom of God? Be not deceived, neither fornicators, nor idolaters, nor adulterers, nor effeminate, nor abusers of themselves with mankind (there were many homosexuals and other perverts in that day); nor thieves, nor covetous, nor drunkards, nor revilers, nor extortioners, shall inherit the kingdom of God." (1 Cor. 6:9-10)

Born Free

Chapter Ten

Born free! To do what?

A thirteen-year-old girl had "had it" with her parents. They were a "problem" to her and had been since she was six. She decided that she would not "take" any more from them. They imposed too many restrictions, gave too much advice.

"They can't keep me in any straight jacket," she kept telling herself. "What do they know about my friends anyway? Who says I can't smoke if I want to? I'm going to decide what time I come in at night, not my mother."

So she mumbled to herself and to her boy friend, now a steady. She soon ran away from home and joined a group of others like herself. Many of them were on drugs and indulged in sex freely with anyone they chose, at any time and any place.

They were that free, so they thought, and laughed at the rest of the world with its restrictions on conduct. They lived by robbery and shoplifting, and avoided arrest most of the time by fooling the police and by lying. They kept telling themselves how free they were, free from the restraints of a system they had learned to hate.

But they had a leader who was a czar, who demanded far more compliance with his orders than her mother had ever exacted of her. The whole gang obeyed him, or else!

She found this out one night when they were staging a raid on a drug store. She was posted as lookout. She told the gang chief that she wouldn't do it—she was scared of the police. He drew a knife on her and asked which she feared most, the police or that knife. She yielded. At fifteen she was on heroin and was pregnant. At seventeen she was dead, a victim of syphilis and drugs.

But she had been "free"—free from apron strings, family lectures, family restraints, and had reveled in it. In her new-found "freedom" she had lived the way she wanted to, but fell into the inevitable trap which she had mistaken for the broad gateway to fun and ease, and she died a horrible death as a result.

How free was this girl really? Or was she in truth a slave—to appetite—to passion—to blind selfishness—to fear, fear of that leader with the knife—fear of leaving the gang, for what would she do for a living if she did leave?

She had hated the system under which she had been born, but now found herself shackled even more by another system, a vicious one, with a leader who would not hesitate to kill.

What she did not know and refused to learn was that a free society, where people really have freedom, is a self-disciplined one. It has to be, or it would die of suicide in the same way this girl did, from sordid living.

Because some individuals are selfish and naturally rebel against any kind of restraint, as a people we place ourselves under self-imposed restrictions, or laws, so that the majority can continue to be free and to permit us to protect ourselves from the vicious few.

Then can we turn our backs on discipline, and denounce laws that protect our freedom, and still live and be happy? What if everyone was free to kill everyone else? What if everyone was free to steal anything at all from everyone else? What if every man was free to violate every woman or girl he met. What if every licentious woman was free to seduce every man, and to steal husbands from wives and break up homes? What if every girl on a date was "fair game" for every boy to despoil at his pleasure? What kind of a society would we have?

There is progress, freedom, and happiness only through self-imposed discipline which is accepted by all concerned, so that we are protected from those who would violate the rights of others.

No one has the right to commit murder.

No one has the right to dispossess others of their property.

No one has the right to injure others with impunity.

Yet it all involves freedom and restraint. Among intelligent humans, "dog-eat-dog" tactics are superseded by law, and the law provides legal punishment for crime.

Conformance with law is the only way to progress. How true this is in the natural world. Nature's laws are immovable and unchangeable, but that very fact is what makes science successful.

Let's talk about going to the moon, for example. The moon speeds through space at a rate of 2,289 miles per hour as it makes its orbit around the earth. The earth travels 66,600 miles per hour in its orbit around the sun. The moon is only 2,159.9 miles in diameter, which is a small target at a distance of 238,855 miles.

Have you ever tried shooting at a moving target? Hard to hit, isn't it? The men who compute the mathematics for sending a missile to the moon have to figure on a target moving at the rate of 2,289 miles per hour, and must shoot from a base, the earth, which is moving at 66,600 miles per hour.

How can they do it? They also must figure on the mean eccentricity of the moon's movement, which is determined on a ratio of 0.05490. What makes it possible for them to so perfectly aim their missile into space that it will meet the moon at the precise point in its orbit which will allow astronauts to land on that orb? Only one thing. The stability and certainty of natural law.

Then what puts men on the moon is *conformance* to law. If they should refuse to conform, the astronauts would spend the rest of their existence wandering in space, probably circling around the sun, but never reaching the moon. Exact science, following exact laws, brings them success. Failure to follow the laws would bring failure.

It is that way in life. In all we do there are both cause and effect. Run two cars into each other and you have a collision. Drink poison and you die. Eat good food, get proper exercise and fresh air and you have health. Live righteously and you receive divine blessings. Defy virtue and you reap disease.

When we say we are free we must mean freedom to live our lives under self-imposed laws which are in the best interest of all. To destroy law and order, and uproot the "establishment" is no more sensible than it would be to ignore the trajectory which would put men on the moon. And to suppose that we can ignore divine law in our personal lives is just as foolhardy.

Born free? Yes, we were born with free agency to make our own choices in life. But each choice is a seed, and each seed produces a harvest. What will your harvest be?

Born Free

Know this, that every soul is free
To choose his life and what he'll be,
For this eternal truth is given,
That God will force no man to heaven.

He'll call, persuade, direct aright,
And bless with wisdom, love and light,
In nameless ways be good and kind,
But never force the human mind.

Freedom and reason make us men;
Take these away, what are we then?
Mere animals, and just as well,
The beasts may think of heaven or hell.

May we no more our powers abuse,
But ways of truth and goodness choose.
Our God is pleased when we improve
His grace and seek his perfect love.

The Sanctity of Sex

Chapter Eleven

Today sex is being made a social football, and in the process it is being dragged into all the filth of perdition. But it was not always so, and among right-thinking people, it still has its proper place.

In reality, sex is something sacred and pure. It has a divine purpose. God made it, and did so as part of his eternal plan for mankind. It is only through the devices of Satan and his followers that many drag it down into degradation and filth.

In the creation God decreed that everything should reproduce itself, whether plant or animal, and it was so. It was part of the creative process, and hence was sacred in its purpose. If there were no reproduction, life would soon cease to exist.

The earth was made as a home for the children of our Father in Heaven, and we are those children. We are the literal offspring of our God, his spirit children. In our pre-existence we became members of his family, just as we became members of our families here on earth. Jesus was the firstborn, and we came afterward. Our destiny is to become like God at some time.

Our spirits live in our bodies of flesh and bone. God has a body of flesh and bones, glorious like that of the Christ after his resurrection. Also like Jesus, the Father is a spirit clothed in flesh. We are spirits clothed in flesh. He is eternal and glorious. We are mortal. But in our resurrection we too may have glorious bodies. In order for us to become like our Heavenly Father, two things were necessary:

One was that we obtain a body of flesh and bones because he has such a body, and without it we could not become like him.

The other was that we were to be tested and tried to prove our worthiness to be like him, and in this life such a testing was planned.

Hence, it was necessary for us to come to this earth. Adam and Eve were placed here first, and were commanded to reproduce themselves. This they did through sex, as other life did. It was God's means of reproduction, and it was pure.

Reproduction for human kind, however, is different from that in other forms of life, because the human line of descent provides bodies for the children of God. Since he desired that all of his children be well-born, he placed safeguards about the human act of reproduction, and therefore gave us both marriage and the law of chastity.

Only within legal marriage may children be born with the blessing of God. These children, being his own, have a right to be well born, and hence should come to earth only through properly married parents.

Sex is so sacred to the Lord that anciently he decreed the death penalty for transgressors of the law of chastity. In our day sinners are handled by Church courts and if unrepentant are excommunicated.

When sex is used in the way the Lord designed, those participating in the act become joint creators with God. To profane this act, then becomes one of the worst sins in the Lord's category of transgression.

The worst of all sins is that against the Holy Ghost. Next comes murder, wherein we shed innocent blood and then comes sex sin. There is no forgiveness for the first two offenses, but the Lord has decreed that persons who have committed sex sins may be forgiven if they completely repent and reform their lives, keeping his commandments.

Lucifer seeks to destroy the fountains of life. He has inspired the world to place a demoralizing emphasis upon sex. It is in the movies, the magazines, the styles, radio programs, and even in conversation.

And what is the purpose of this emphasis? It is to embarrass the Creator, degrade the pure act of reproduction, and make it common and cheap—a plaything. How Satan must laugh when we fall into his vicious trap!

Parenthood is next to Godhood, it has been said. Certainly it is part of the divine act of creation. But it must always respect the restrictions which the Lord has placed about it; otherwise, it becomes an abomination.

Some of our Church leaders have said that they would rather see their own children dead and in their graves—clean—than to have them live unclean lives. Virtue is more important than the preservation of life. Protect it above your life!

No Trial Marriages

Chapter Twelve

Trial marriage, of one kind or another, has been urged periodically for many generations. Always it has been advocated as a means of reducing the frightening increase in divorce.

There is no such thing as a "trial marriage", either under the law of man or God. Marriage is only a marriage when performed under license by proper authority recognized by the law.

Marriage in no sense can be either a trial or an experiment. It is intended to be permanent with full acceptance of the responsibilities thereof, and not to be abandoned at any slight provocation.

But in case there were such a thing as a trial marriage, what kind of a relationship would it be? It would and could only be a case of two unmarried people living together in an adulterous relationship. It could not be anything else in a respectable, law-abiding society, and those who advocate it, as even some clergymen are now doing, are simply attempting to foist a vicious practice upon the unsuspecting public.

Adultery and fornication never have been deterrants to divorce. Rather, they have been prime CAUSES of divorce, for they multiply infidelity and encourage promiscuity among both young and old.

When did illicit sex acts ever establish stability, either of character or of home and family life? Always they have done the direct opposite, and have broken more hearts and more homes than any other one thing, even more than liquor or quarreling over money.

Such relationships always add to promiscuity, with deluded people going from one sex partner to another, no longer feeling any responsibility to any of them, and regarding them only as a convenience or a toy. And to be even more frank, what person would want to accept someone else's cast-off for further trial "marriages" except the promiscuous and the perverts?

In the language of the scripture, pre-marital sex (to use the modern polite term) is nothing more nor less than fornication, one of the three worst sins in the Lord's category of crime. No Latter-day Saint should ever allow himself or herself to be so deluded and misled as to believe that any sex act is allowed by the Lord prior to or outside of legal marriage.

Today's world loses sight of the true meaning of marriage. God himself gave it in the first place, marrying Adam and Eve in a HOLY union. It was intended to be eternal, for God's mode of marriage is eternal, surviving both death and the resurrection.

When the Savior spoke of divorce in his day, based on the practice introduced by Moses, he said, "Moses, because of the hardness of your hearts, suffered you to put away your wives. BUT FROM THE BEGINNING IT WAS NOT SO." (Matt. 19:8)

God provided marriage in the beginning (and he does not change) to set up a family relationship on the earth WHICH CAN BE PROJECTED INTO ETERNITY. He has his form or mode of marriage, just as he has his mode of baptism. His marriage is temple marriage. It is a divine form which will continue with us in this life and through death and the resurrection into our exaltation in the eternal world.

Exaltation in eternity comes only to those married in the temple, and to no one else. The Lord, of course, is fair and just to all, and will give to every righteous person the opportunity to receive all of his saving blessings. But some reject the privilege of temple marriage probably not understanding it when they do so.

The gospel is spoken of as being in two divisions, with one set of commandments referring to the living of the good life, and a second equally important set of commands referring to the ordinances of the gospel.

All of the ordinances are necessary to our exaltation in the kingdom of Heaven. It will be remembered that when the Lord talked with Nicodemus he told this leader among the Jews that unless he was baptized he could not even see the Kingdom of Heaven (John 3). Not even his righteousness would save him without baptism, for without it he could not even SEE heaven. It is that way with all saving ordinances of the gospel.

The ordinances likewise may be spoken of as being in two classes, one set which may be performed OUT of the temple, and the other set which is reserved for sacred houses specially built and dedicated for that purpose. But in or out of the temple, the saving ordinances are ALL essential to our exaltation.

The temple ordinances, then, are SAVING ordinances in the same sense in which baptism is. We can no more be exalted in the celestial kingdom without temple marriage than we could without baptism, lacking which Nicodemus could not even see the kingdom. Of those who reject temple marriage, knowing its significance, the Lord has said:

> "When they are out of the world they neither marry nor are given in marriage; but are appointed angels in heaven, which angels are MINISTERING SERVANTS to minister for those who are worthy of a far more, and an exceeding, and an eternal weight of glory."

So then we see that those rejecting temple marriage, but otherwise worthy to enter into some other portion of the Lord's kingdom, are to be servants, to wait upon the needs of those who are exalted. But is this just?

We are all judged according to our deeds in the flesh. God's judgments are always just. As to these "servants" or "angels", he has said:

> "For these angels did not abide my law; therefore, they cannot be enlarged, but remain SEPARATELY AND SINGLY (without marriage) WITHOUT EXALTATION, in their saved condition—TO ALL ETERNITY." (D.&C. 132:16-17)

Temple marriage is that important, and this fact many young people seem not to understand, or they would make any sacrifice to obtain it.

The Lord taught the same doctrine in Section 131 of the Doctrine and Covenants, in which we read:

> "In the celestial glory there are three heavens or degrees, and in order to obtain the highest a man must enter into this order of the priesthood (meaning the new and everlasting covenant of marriage), and if he does not he cannot obtain it. He may enter into the other, but that is the end of his kingdom; he cannot have an increase."

There is a frightening finality about this language, as is the case with that quoted from Section 132 above. So just as truly as Nicodemus could not enter the kingdom without water baptism, neither can we, nor Nicodemus, nor anyone else, receive exaltation without temple marriage.

It is the law of God which none of us can circumvent. Such marriage, which prepares us for exaltation, of necessity is based upon complete chastity and virtue, for no unclean thing can enter into his presence.

Could a trial marriage, no matter what it is called, ever lead to such a blessing, since trial marriage literally is pre-marital sex, which is fornication? Can free sex in any form receive other than the condemnation of the Almighty?

President David O. McKay said:

> Happiness does not begin at the altar; it begins during the period of youth and courtship. These seeds of happiness are sown by one's ability to master his driving passion. Chastity should be the dominant virtue among young people.
>
> Some young couples enter into marriage and procrastinate bringing children into their homes. They are running a great risk. Marriage is for the purpose of rearing a family, and youth is the time to do it. I admire these young mothers with four or five children around them now, still young and happy. Failure to rear a family is one of the conditions that cause love to wilt and eventually to die.

There are some persons who have resisted temple marriage, and accepted a civil ceremony only, because they have said they did not want to be sealed for eternity until they had lived together long enough to know if they really want each other hereafter. Doesn't this place even civil marriage on a trial basis?

Marriage—initially—in the temple is what is taught by the leaders of the Church. Temple marriage should not be placed in a secondary position at any time. When can God's law ever be made of secondary importance?

Civil marriage is man's mode of marriage. Temple marriage is God's mode. We should be no more willing to accept man's mode of marriage than we would accept man's mode of baptism. Would any one of us feel good about a baptism at the hands of some sectarian minister who had no divine authority, and could not give our baptism an eternal significance?

There is no more ETERNAL significance to a marriage which lasts only "until death do you part" than there is to an unauthorized baptism.

Whom Shall We Date?

Chapter Thirteen

Since temple marriage is essential to our exaltation, and since only faithful Latter-day Saints can enter the temple, by simple deduction we come to the conclusion that Latter-day Saints should marry Latter-day Saints, with both parties worthy to enter the temple and receive its saving ordinances.

That also would seem to limit the field as to dating practices. Normally we marry those with whom we date. We marry our friends, not strangers. Then if we hope to be exalted, and therefore plan on a temple marriage which is a gateway to exaltation, with whom should we date? Obviously, those who would be eligible to accompany us through the temple.

Is this something new? Was such a law known anciently? Again, has the Lord changed? It is of more than ordinary interest to see how the Lord protected his people anciently from being "unequally yoked together" with unbelievers, and his reasons for it. He was most plain in his instructions, as he is today.

Said Paul:

"Be ye not unequally yoked together with unbelievers, for what fellowship hath righteousness with unrighteousness? And what communion hath light with darkness? And what concord hath Christ with Belial, or what part hath he that believeth with an infidel?

"And what agreement hath the temple of God with idols, for ye are the temple of God; as God hath said, I will dwell in them, and walk in them, and I will be their God, and they shall be my people.

"Wherefore come out from among them, and be ye SEPARATE, saith the Lord, and touch not the unclean thing, and I will receive you, and will be a Father unto you, and ye shall be my sons and daughters, saith the Almighty." (2 Cor. 6:14-18)

When speaking to ancient Israel about their unbelieving neighbors, the Lord said:

"Neither shalt thou make marriages with them; thy daughter thou shalt not give unto his son; nor his daughter shalt thou take unto thy son."

And then he gives his strong reasons in this language:

"FOR THEY WILL TURN AWAY THY SON FROM FOLLOWING ME, that they may serve other gods. So will the anger of the Lord be kindled against you and destroy thee suddenly." (Deut. 7)

In numerous other instances was this doctrine taught. It will be remembered how Abraham endeavored to choose a BELIEVING wife for Isaac, and how Isaac did the same thing regarding his son Jacob, SO THAT THERE WOULD BE A UNITY OF RELIGION IN THE FAMILY AND SO THAT CHILDREN MIGHT BE REARED IN THE FAITH.

It is the same today. Mixed marriages—those of believers and unbelievers—have similar problems, and perpetuate all the ills of mixed marriages anciently. Usually they end up in one of the following categories:

1—A "truce" may be declared between the two parties, each one going to his or her own church. This preserves disunity, and raises severe problems for the children. Whose religion will they take, the mother's or the father's?

2—One spouse converts the other spouse, thus uniting the family in the same faith. But this is rare. Statistics indicate that this takes place in only one in eight cases.

3—The family gives up all religion to prevent a break in the home. This results in children being raised without any religion. Is this common? About 45 per cent of the total population of the United States belongs to no church whatever, with the children in those homes being reared without religious instruction. This condition contributes largely to our present moral collapse, because when the restraint of religion is taken away, sinning becomes easy, and is not regarded as being serious.

4—Divorce results because the spouses refuse to give up their own religion, and refuse to yield in any way to the persuasions of the other party to the marriage. A high percentage of marriages between devout religious persons end in divorce because of this situation.

With these facts before us, it is easy to understand the Lord's point of view. He seeks to preserve religious unity among his people; otherwise, his people would cease to exist AS A PEOPLE. They and their faith would be diluted to the point of ineffectiveness.

He is establishing his kingdom on the earth. He builds it upon the united faith of a united people. He has said (1 Cor. 1) that Christ is not divided.

Jesus taught that a house divided against itself will fall. (Matt. 12:25) He said that his kingdom is one with a strait gate and a narrow way, adding that unfortunately "few there be that find it." (Matt. 7:13)

To be forewarned, it is said, is to be forearmed. Then what should our attitude be? If we love the Lord, we will obey his commands. "He that hath my commandments and keepeth them, he it is that loveth me." (John 14:31-24).

Being "in the world but not of the world," it is difficult at times to resist the impulse to date people not of our faith. At times we live in places where Latter-day Saints are in the extreme minority, and where religion has not been made important in the lives of our friends. Many of them have no interest at all in religion. Naturally, this would come from the 45 per cent of homes having no religious affiliation.

Dr. James Clayton, University of Utah history professor, told a panel conducted at the University Union Building that youth is at an age where there is always the least commitment to religious belief. He quoted statistics which indicated that 58 per cent of the nation's college students find that religion has very little relevance in their lives.

Again this is not surprising, since 45 per cent of all homes in the nation have no church affiliation. Usually, in religious as well as political matters, "as it is with the parents, so it is with the children."

But knowing this, Latter-day Saints are forewarned and put on their guard. To them the gospel is the most important thing in life. All other things become subservient to the Lord and his purposes, and when we know that he requires temple marriage of us, we should plan for it, and so choose our friends that we will marry within the Church and within the temple, and not be "unequally yoked together with unbelievers."

Short Skirts—Long Hair

Chapter Fourteen

They are cousins! Did you know?

They both spring from the same over-all source, and are symbols of the same dangerous situation.

Teens of this day will not remember the months following World War II, but during that period a revolution began which is only now coming into full bloom. It was not a political revolt; it was moral. It was spawned by that war, and broke down standards which had been held sacred from time immemorial.

Will you take time to read a little history? It affects you directly, and will help you make some vital decisions.

That moral revolution was very slow getting under way. It met with much resistance. It takes a tremendous effort to break down good character and high standards, so the change came slowly, but it was relentless nevertheless.

In World War II many women joined the army, navy, air force and the marines. They didn't face the enemy, nor did they fire any guns, but they filled many assignments which released men to go into battle.

They drove cars, did office work, served as orderlies, and of course thousands were nurses.

Nurses are always regarded as angels of mercy, which indeed they are, and many have given their lives in field hospitals while extending care to the wounded that only a merciful woman can give.

But when their sister recruits began driving trucks and jeeps, and when they earned commissions forcing the non-commissioned men in the service to salute female lieutenants, captains and majors, their status changed, and with it a new attitude was born, both among men and women alike.

This, in turn, changed standards, moral and otherwise, and soon put women in an entirely new light. If women were going to be like men, and do their jobs and enjoy their "rights and privileges", why shouldn't they come off their high pedestals and indulge like men, it was asked.

Many of the women themselves had this idea, and began to demand rights that previously had been restricted to men. Taking advantage of this, the cigaret makers saw no reason why cigarets should not be sold to the hosts of women the world over. They would form a new and profitable market. So a campaign was begun to induce them to smoke.

Hitting at an easy target the cigaret merchants settled on the issue of weight control, and told women everywhere that they would stay thin if they smoked cigarets. This, of course, interested millions, for what girl doesn't want to be thin and sylph-like?

The appeal was to "reach for a cigaret instead of a sweet," implying that the use of cigarets would improve one's health. This campaign continued until the government stopped it because of its false advertising.

During this time women were portrayed frequently in cigaret advertising, but not at first in the act of smoking. When the ads appeared showing women actually holding cigarets in their hands, a revulsion came, and the cigaret advertisers had to back down for a time.

But step by step they dulled the sensibilities of decent people, until finally pictures were commonly published showing women in the act of smoking. The models chosen for this advertising, of course, were beautiful, and the surroundings in which the pictures were taken were attractive. It was made to appear that surely, smoking really was THE thing to do.

Then came liquor. To induce women to drink, the name "saloon" was dropped, and drinking places became known as taverns, and later still, to gain an even greater appearance of respectability, they were called lounges. Liquor was popularized for meal time, for parties, for business gatherings.

Soon drinking became a matter of social status with many people. It was THE thing to do. Women soon were both smoking and drinking almost as much as men. The clever campaign moved fast as more and more became gullible about anything that seemed fashionable. Until that time few women would have considered stooping to the point of participating in a drinking party or being seen on the street with a cigaret.

For a long time they had been on a pedestal, placed there by men who respected them and who expected superior moral conduct from them. The purity of women was still a maxim to most men, and they defended it.

But now the campaign destroyed all that and down came the standards. Evil men began to look more and more upon women as conveniences and playthings. As women lowered their own standards, these men adjusted their estimate of women in direct ratio, and removed them from the pedestals which had protected them for so long from predatory lusts.

Many women then set aside the femininity which had sustained them previously. In doing so they seemed to admit that indeed they were the playthings lustful men said they were.

Then came the "sex appeal" gimmick. Everything had to have "sex appeal"—dress, cars, home furnishings—everything! It became the theme in nearly all advertising.

Women, some well dressed and some only scantily clothed, began appearing in ads for everything from perfume to automobile tires. It was carried to ridiculous extremes. But because the mere mention of sex did appeal to many, the campaign moved on.

But then it was found that sex appeal was not really effective unless it DISPLAYED sex. So the mini-skirt was born, first to the disgust of most people, but soon to be accepted world-wide.

Did its appearance have any significant effect? Sex crimes skyrocketed. Even in staid old Japan the mini-skirt appeared and with it, during the first year, forcible rape increased 400 per cent in Tokyo alone. It was more than that in some American cities.

Women seem not to realize it, but they cannot expose their bodies without tempting some men, although a good many more are simply disgusted. But mini-skirts were stylish, and if this was the price of fashion, so be it. This seemed to be the attitude. Women took the moral risk in the name of fashion.

Then the promoters of unchastity began discussing sex acts openly in magazines and newspapers, and movies capped it all with sensual films. Next came the "pill" and other contraceptives, making the gullible feel that they could sin and not pay the price. Since they no longer feared pregnancy, promiscuity spread.

Some educators, and even some clergymen endorsed it. Movies brazenly and fearlessly displayed the most carnal sex scenes on the screen. Pornographic books and magazines became best sellers. But the inevitable happened, and venereal disease raised its head with awesome results. Regardless, the sex craze went on.

Night clubs began the fad of "topless" waitresses and dancers; then competition forced them to go "bottomless" and then to "topless and bottomless." At last they spoke openly of "nudies."

Some legislatures joined the parade by legalizing prostitution for sixteen-year-olds, and homosexuality for all consenting parties. We seemed to plunge into a bottomless pit of sensuality.

Then came the "hot" music. The Beatles were first to make it popular, and since they "caught on" so widely their appearance as well as their music became popular. Standards—of a kind—were set by them, and the "sheep" blindly followed.

Rock music, appealing to the baser instincts, brought with it a new theme in lyrics for the songs, a sensual, suggestive, vile line. Since the Beatles were so popular, many young fellows thought it was smart to dress like them, and so long hair came into the picture.

Many boys, no doubt free from evil motives, grew long hair just to be in the new style, as many good girls wore revealing mini-skirts and tight pants for the same reason. They HAD to be in style!

Then came the hippie element, adding another dimension to the degradation that was heaping up.

And because hippies received much publicity, even their styles attained a certain popularity.

Next came the drug invasion. It seemed only necessary to tell certain people that something—anything—was the thing to do, and they would accept it, even if it killed them.

And hundreds were killed by drugs, many went insane, and hosts of others suffered side effects which will not only hamper them for the rest of their lives, but may bring physical deformities upon many innocent children, born as addicts from their mothers' wombs, having been fed the poisons through the blood stream.

That is the history. It is not pretty. Only a return to common sense can restore healthful living and decency.

Little can be said for the mini-skirt or "hot pants" if modesty is the subject. Everyone admits they are suggestive in the extreme. Sad it is that many girls actually seem to enjoy the exposure, obviously being unashamed. But while short skirts have little, if any defense, some do raise an argument in favor of long hair. Is there anything immoral about long hair, they ask.

Advocates of long hair point to pictures of Brigham Young and other pioneers, and some even mention the Savior, and say, if there is anything so bad about long hair, what about them? The same question might be asked about other things too.

For a long time, for example, the little game of bingo was a child's harmless toy, with no stigma of any kind attached to it. But when bingo became a major GAMBLING device the connotation changed completely. It was not the game, in and of itself, that was bad. IT WAS ITS USE AND ASSOCIATION. Gambling is always bad, and when any device, ever so harmless by itself, is used as a means of gambling, immediately it acquires a stigma.

It is the same with long hair. In the days of the Savior there were very few barbers, as all will admit, and hair styling for men was an unknown art. It was not too different with Brigham Young and the pioneers. Where were the barber shops along the trail across the plains, or in the rugged frontier villages which they built?

Could it have been that the pioneers were so busily engaged in building a new life in the unconquered west that they had little time to worry about the appearance of their hair?

Obviously in that day there was no association between bad morals and hair styling that could possibly place any stigma on long hair. As regards the Savior, who knows how he looked? All we have in any picture of him is some artist's conception of his appearance. Who knows whether he wore long hair or short hair? The Apostle Paul said that men in that day wore short hair (1 Cor. 14).

But today it is different. BY ASSOCIATION long hair has become a symbol of the moral revolt which has brought in the hippies, rock music, drugs and low sex acts. It is that association which makes it repulsive. Long hair today is associated with the rock groups and all they stand for. It is related to drug abuse and to hippies. It is a symbol of low moral standards, and a rejection of virtue and good taste.

What true "Mormon" boy or girl would knowingly become a symbol of a sex revolt or of drug abuse, or of widespread promiscuity? When we associate with evil, it rubs off on us. When we walk in filth it sticks to us. By association respectable things become disreputable, and clean things dragged in the gutter become repulsive.

The path of wisdom is in profiting by the mistakes of others and following a direct line of righteousness. History tells us how, and the history of the sex revolt in particular should persuade every one of us that there is no happiness in any kind of sin, but only degradation.

Happiness is a product of righteous living.

Like Men or Like Women?

Chapter Fifteen

"Is that a boy or a girl?"

How often has that question been asked as we have watched a slim, long-haired person wearing a string of beads walking down the street! When girls wear men's clothes and boys wear long hair and beads, it is difficult to tell at times whether they are of the masculine or feminine gender. And is this good?

Bishop Victor L. Brown of the Presiding Bishopric raised this question in an address during a General Conference of the Church, and said:

"In the Scriptures we read, 'So God created man in his own image, in the image of God created he him, male and female created he them.'

"The Lord defined some very basic differences between men and women. He gave the male what we call masculine traits, and the female feminine traits. He did not intend either of the sexes to adopt the other's traits, but rather, that men should look and act like men and that women should look like and act like women. When these differences are ignored, an unwholesome relationship develops which, if not checked, can lead to the reprehensible, tragic sin of homosexuality. In other words, we have a responsibility to be examples of true manhood or womanhood.

"The Lord commanded men and women to multiply and replenish the earth. 'And God blessed them, and God said unto them, be fruitful, and multiply, and replenish the earth, and subdue it: and have dominion over the fish of the sea, and the fowl of the air, and over living thing that moveth upon the earth.' (Genesis 1:28) To insure that this would take place, he gave to each a powerful emotion which caused a male and a female to be attracted to each other.

"To them he gave a mind with which to reason, so that they might have dominion over 'every living thing that moveth upon the earth.' With this in mind he also expects mankind to have dominion over himself. He expects us to exercise control over our sexual desires. Sexual activity is to be indulged in only within the bounds of marriage. When this is the case, it is one of the most rewarding and satisfying experiences man can have.

"When this is not the case, the same experience becomes base and evil. Notwithstanding the attitude of much of the world towards sexual permissiveness, the Lord has never changed his commandment in this regard. He said, 'Thou shalt not commit adultery.' (Exodus 20:14) Infidelity and promiscuous sexual activity destroy the basic, vital institution of the family which in turn destroys all that is good in life.

"If we as priesthood holders are to bring honor to that priesthood, we will refrain from any sexual activity outside the bonds of matrimony. Otherwise, we bring disgrace to ourselves and to the priesthood we bear.

"Acknowledgment of the fact that this mortal body is the tabernacle of the spirit and that the spirit was fathered by our Father in Heaven, behooves us to show respect for our bodies by not abusing them through the use of harmful and destructive substances."

The Apostle Paul spoke at length concerning the man's appearance, and that of a woman, and emphasized that each should keep his or her own place. In his epistle to the Corinthians he pointed this out (1 Cor. 14), and among other things said:

"Doth not even nature itself teach you that if a man have long hair it is a shame unto him?" (v. 14), this coming after a long discussion of what a man may do and wear and what a woman should likewise do and wear. It may be argued that this was merely a custom in Paul's day, but nevertheless the whole tenor of both history and scripture emphasizes that man should be masculine and woman should be feminine.

The Generation Gap
Chapter Sixteen

One of the main complaints of errant young people is against their own parents. They feel that the home is too strict, that parents are too demanding, and that father and mother do not understand the youth. Many say that every young person should be at liberty to choose his own way of life. But is this so? Are young people—just growing up—possessed of sufficient wisdom to know how to cope with the conflicts of this present world? And if so, whence this wisdom?

It is well for young and old alike to pause and ask themselves what the Lord said about this matter. He is all wise. His inspired word is available to us. Should there be any conflict between the generations?

It is admitted that in this day the plight of many young people is traceable directly to the inadequacy of their own homes. The mistakes of parents are perpetuated and expanded in their children. These mistakes do create gulfs or gaps in many families, it is true.

But if parents would teach their children in righteousness, and if children would listen in righteousness, there would be no generation gaps and no conflicts in the family.

Most young people are good and most parents are sincere and earnest in wishing to do their best for their children. Errors in judgment should not be allowed to condemn the efforts of well-meaning parents or children.

Few parents are really evil in their intent toward their children; very few are deliberately cruel. How many mothers have worked their fingers to the bone to provide for their children! How many fathers have taken two or three jobs at a time to bring home the necessary means for the family!

And yet in these very homes, there are conflicts between the generations. Most of them, however, come back to one thing: selfishness. Demanding children may be as unjust as demanding parents. From such conditions as these, misunderstandings arise which we call the generation gap.

The Lord never intended that there should be a generation gap. He taught the greatest of cohesiveness in family life. He taught that parents must honor their children and do well by them, but he likewise taught that children must honor their parents in righteousness. From whence came the commandment:

"Honor thy father and thy mother that thy days may be long upon the land which the Lord thy God giveth thee"? (Exodus 20)

If we believe in God, should we not obey his counsel? Can we say that our parents are not worthy of honor? It may be that some are not. But even so, they are our parents and are worthy of our gratitude at least for giving us our lives and that is a most important item, as all will agree.

God decrees that we honor our parents, and in the commandment made no exceptions for the dishonorable

Shall I Force My Child

by J. Edgar Hoover

Shall I make my child go to Sunday School and Church? Yes! And with no further discussion about the matter. Startled? Why? How do you answer Junior when he comes to breakfast on Monday morning and announces to you that he is not going to school any more? You know! Junior goes.

How do you answer when Junior comes in very much besmudged and says, "I'm not going to take a bath." Junior bathes, doesn't he?

Why all this timidity, then, in the realm of his spiritual guidance and growth? Going to let him wait and decide what Church he'll go to when he's old enough? Quit your kidding! You didn't wait until you were old enough. You don't wait until he is old enough to decide whether he wants to go to school or not to start his education. You don't wait until he is old enough to decide whether he wants to be clean or dirty, do you? Do you wait until he is old enough to decide if he wants to take his medicine when he is sick, do you?

What shall we say when Junior announces he doesn't like to go to Sunday School and Church? That's an easy one to answer. Just be consistent. Tell him, "Junior, in our house we all go to church and to Sunday School, and that includes you." Your firmness and example will furnish a bridge over which youthful rebellion may travel into rich and satisfying experience in personal religious living. The parents of America can strike a telling blow against the forces that contribute to our juvenile delinquency, if our mothers and fathers will take their children to Sunday School and Church regularly.

ones. And when he taught parents to care for their children he made no exception for wayward ones, who need parental care even more than others.

He gives two commandments: One to parents to teach their children, and the second to children to honor their parents. Without reservations of any kind, without allowances for special cases, he gives these commands. It is for us, as believers in the Almighty, to obey.

Some young people resent being "forced" to go to school or to church. Are they right in their resentment? It is admitted that the methods used by parents may vary, and that some are more kind than others.

But as to the principle that children should be trained, there can be no doubt. Of course, that training should be given intelligently and with kindness and understanding. All will admit that. And yet parents who give that training are no more perfect than children who receive it.

Was there ever any training without discipline?

And yet, it is training which develops skill and opens the door to achievement. Is not a good doctor a well-trained man? Is not the great architect or the great construction engineer a well-trained man? And what of the great musicians? Are they not well taught and carefully trained? And did not each one submit to the rigorous discipline which the training required of him?

In war, well-trained soldiers win the victories. It is well known that the greatest number of casualties in battle are among the poorest trained troops. And what develops the best training? Discipline. What could be said of the wisdom of a soldier who had refused the training which a well-disciplined course would provide, and who would go into battle unprepared for combat.

Is he wise to resent the very thing which would preserve his life and give him victory on the battlefield?

Yet such training is based fully on discipline. The soldier learns to OBEY the rules of safety and success. That is where the discipline comes in. Is it any different with life? Isn't life a battle in a very real sense? Then dare we enter the field without preparation? And can we obtain that preparation without the guidance of experienced teachers who have been over the road and who know each curve and rut and hazard?

It is wise to take counsel from those who know. As Joseph Smith said, "No one can be saved in ignorance." To spurn knowledge and wisdom—to resist experienced direction—is folly in the extreme.

Is it any wonder then that the Lord provided a means for us to learn from our elders how best to meet life and succeed in it? That is why he gave us parents and Church leaders. There is no substitute for experience, and we learn from those who have it. That is why youth should honor their elders in righteousness, and willingly—even eagerly—learn from them. Would anyone knowing the facts resent such assistance? Would any apprentice resent the advice of a master craftsman?

Young people cannot suppose in this day of "liberation" that parental guidance is bad. If they do so, they fly in the face of Providence, for it is God who provides such guidance and not only does he provide it, but he also commands it! Note what the Lord said about parents teaching their children the gospel truths:

"And again, inasmuch as parents have children in Zion, or in any of her stakes which are organized, that teach them not to understand the doctrines of repentance, faith in Christ, the Son of the living God, and of baptism and the gift of the

Holy Ghost by the laying on of the hands, when eight years old, the sin be upon the heads of the parents.
"For this shall be a law unto the inhabitants of Zion, or in any of her stakes which are organized.
"And their children shall be baptized for the remission of their sins when eight years old, and receive the laying on of the hands.
"And they shall also teach their children to pray, and to walk uprightly before the Lord." (D&C 68:25-28)

This same truth has been taught by the Lord's prophets through all time. For example, the Apostle Paul wrote:

"Wives, submit yourselves unto your husbands, as it is fit in the Lord.
"Husbands, love your wives, and be not bitter against them.
"Children, obey your parents in all things: for this is well pleasing unto the Lord.
"Fathers, provoke not your children to anger, lest they be discouraged." (Colossians 3:18-21)

And, of course, Solomon, the wise man of ancient time, said much on this subject. Note a few of his teachings:

"Train up a child in the way he should go: and when he is old, he will not depart from it." (Proverbs 22:6)
"The fear of the Lord is the beginning of knowledge: but fools despise wisdom and instruction.
"My son, hear the instruction of thy father, and forsake not the law of thy mother . . ." (Proverbs 1:7-8)

He applied the same principle to our relationship with God, who is also our Father, when he said:

"My son, despise not the chastening of the Lord; neither be weary of his correction:
For whom the Lord loveth he correcteth; even as a father the son in whom he delighteth." (Proverbs 3:9-12)

God disciplines us because he wants to train us to become like him. But can we become like him without a learning process? And can there be a learning process without the necessary discipline to protect us from going off on tangents which could bring us to destruction?

And can we have an effective learning process without a teacher?

Then there need be no generation gap between parents and children. If both will recognize the positions in which God places them and in righteousness follow the divine plan, both will succeed, understanding will prevail, and there will always be love at home.

A New Significance

Chapter Seventeen

God is all-wise and provides well for our needs. We in turn show our wisdom when we accept his guidance.

One of the most important revelations he has given us for our well being is the Word of Wisdom. This is especially evident now, when it seems that almost every conceivable stimulant is paraded before us in enticing ways.

In this day of drug abuse, the Word of Wisdom takes on a new and greater significance, and should make every alert Latter-day Saint feel more grateful than ever for the timely warnings of the Gospel.

The Lord advises us against artificial stimulants. Such commodities are not listed by name in the Word of Wisdom, for that revelation still stands as it was given At that time the Prophet Joseph defined tea and coffee as the hot drinks referred to.

But the leaders of the Church of today have advised, and do presently advise, against the use of anything containing harmful habit-forming drugs under circumstances that would result in the acquiring of the habit.

They advise that anything contaning ingredients that are harmful to the body should be avoided.

Such advice has direct application to the present day abuse of drugs which are consumed now by many young people.

Some students take drugs to keep them awake at night while they study; then on retiring they take other drugs to put them to sleep, and take still others next morning to make them alert.

At examination time they take more drugs, supposedly to quicken their intellects so that they will do well on their tests. Then, keyed up as they are, they need relaxants, and so they take still more. It is a vicious circle.

Many young people, completely misled by what they think is the popular thing to do, appear to be innocently led into a trap and thus become addicted before they know what is taking place.

The addiction comes about through an approach quite different from, and in no way related to, the type of addiction which is known to the "hippie" element in our population, but is just as deadly.

When Art Linkletter's daughter began taking the drugs which led to her death, she did not do it with any evil intent. She was innocently trapped into that situation, but it killed her nevertheless.

Hosts of other young people have had similar experiences. Many die every week in this nation, the victims of drugs, most of them having adopted the habit innocently.

There is the element of a "thrill" to the drug habit also, and this also misleads young people. Like drinking liquor, smoking cigarets, and more recently promiscuity, many have indulged for the "thrill"; some have done it on a dare, but all apparently thinking that it is a part of the young adult life of today.

But the "thrill" invariably turns into distress. It often leads to insanity and degradation. The habit is not easily overcome. Ask anyone who has become its slave.

Our medical advisors constantly say that the body is not benefited in any way by stimulants which drive it beyond its normal capacity. Pep pills take away vitality, they do not add to it. The body must pay for each stimulant it absorbs.

What appears to be a temporary "lift" becomes a loan from the reservoir of energy which must be paid back, either in rehabilitation or in illness.

In the first instance it is like obtaining a loan from a bank. In the second, it is like going into bankruptcy, physically and mentally, which means illness and possibly death.

If we live the Word of Wisdom and avoid the pitfalls against which our leaders warn us, we shall still "run and not be weary and shall walk and not faint" and the destroying angel will pass by us, and not slay us.

Indeed the Word of Wisdom has a new and added significance today.

The Devil Is A Liar!

Chapter Eighteen

The scriptures teach that the Devil is a liar, and has been from the beginning.

But he is not the only one, for he endeavors to persuade all else to become like himself. With many he succeeds abundantly, much to his own gratification. In speaking of this propensity, the Lord says of the Devil:

"He saith unto them, deceive and lie in wait to catch, that ye may destroy; behold this is no harm. And thus he flattereth them and telleth them that it is no sin to lie that they may catch a man in a lie, that they may destroy him.

"And thus he flattereth them and leadeth them along until he draggeth their souls down to hell, and thus he causeth them to catch themselves in their own snare." (D&C 10:24-28)

Since dishonesty, insincerity and a passion to "save face" have become such a part of our modern way of life, this scripture brings a timely warning.

As criminality has soared, so has lying to cover up dishonesty. Deceit, misrepresentation of facts, and scheming for our own aggrandizement, are all part of the same package.

Lying is as despicable as is stealing. Often they are the same, for in lying, people's good names are often stolen away. It is a vicious form of character assassination. This is particularly true in such cases as are referred to in the above-mentioned scripture, where people tell lies in an effort to destroy another person.

Cheating in school is one of the common forms of dishonesty today. And what if students carry this into their careers?

How would you like to be operated upon by a doctor who had cheated his way through medical school, or how would you like to fly in a plane piloted by a man who had cheated his way through flight training?

Successful careers depend upon honest effort. Cheating our way through school can only handicap ourselves and jeopardize others—even their lives under some circumstances.

Take honesty out of our effort and we make our work dishonorable! Can anything be dishonest and honorable at the same time? Is the slothful worker honorable? Is the "don't care" craftsman honest? Does his work stand up? Do his repairs have to be redone? Does he take more time on the job than he should? Does he pad his time card?

Work is honorable if the job is done honestly, but otherwise it is a reflection and an embarrassment.

It would be well worthwhile to every person to take a leaf out of the book of one of our great industrialists:

"I believe that a man's word should be as good as his bond; that character—not wealth nor power nor position—is of supreme worth." (John D. Rockefeller)

It was work that made America great. To suppose now that idleness can make us greater is one of the fallacies of the century. Less work and more play can be the seed of destruction for this nation. The idle mind is still the Devil's workshop.

Honesty

"HONESTY AND SINCERITY ARE THE BASIC VIRTUES OF A NOBLE CHARACTER. HONESTY . . . IS THE FIRST VIRTUE MENTIONED IN THE THIRTEENTH ARTICLE OF FAITH. IT IS FOUNDED ON THE FIRST PRINCIPLES OF HUMAN SOCIETY AND IS THE FOUNDATION PRINCIPLE OF MORAL MANHOOD. *IT IS IMPOSSIBLE TO ASSOCIATE MANHOOD WITH DISHONESTY.* TO BE JUST WITH ONE'S SELF AND TO OTHERS, ONE MUST BE HONEST WITH HIMSELF AND WITH OTHERS.

"THIS MEANS HONESTY IN SPEECH AS WELL AS IN ACTIONS. IT MEANS TO AVOID TELLING HALF TRUTHS AS WELL AS UNTRUTHS. IT MEANS THAT WE ARE HONEST IN OUR DEALINGS—OUR BUYING AS WELL AS OUR SELLING. IT MEANS THAT AN HONEST DEBT CAN NEVER BE OUTLAWED AND THAT A MAN'S WORD IS BETTER THAN HIS BOND. IT MEANS THAT WE WILL BE HONEST IN OUR DEALINGS WITH THE LORD, FOR TRUE HONESTY TAKES INTO ACCOUNT THE CLAIMS OF GOD AS WELL AS THOSE OF MAN; IT RENDERS TO GOD THE THINGS THAT ARE GOD'S, AS WELL AS TO MAN THE THINGS THAT ARE MAN'S."

Pres. David O. McKay

It is interesting to see what some of our great leaders have said about work.

Said Thomas A. Edison: "I never did anything worth doing by accident, nor did any of my inventions come by accident. They came by work."

And J. C. Penney: "I believe in hard work. The only kind of luck any man is justified in counting on is hard work. This means sacrifice, persistent effort, and dogged determination."

And Senator Edward W. Brooke put it this way: "The key word to me is work. If a man is working he doesn't have time for riots. He is improving himself, finding a sense of dignity and an involvement in the community."

And Will Rogers—bless him—said: "What the country needs is dirtier finger nails and cleaner minds."

A timely message comes from Norman Vincent Peale in these words:

"People who choose dishonesty go through life dragging invisible chains. Even when they stifle their conscience with rationalizations, something in them is always looking back fearfully, wondering if their wrong-doing is going to catch up with them. They are trapped in the Land of Look-Behind."

It was God who commanded us to work. It was God who taught us honesty. To steal, to misrepresent, to lie and cheat, are all condemned in his sacred word.

If we are as Christians as we pretend to be, should not every citizen be willing to return to honesty and make it a permanent practice in his life?

Is a relapse into dishonest dealing not an apostasy from fundamental Christianity?

Today's World

Chapter Nineteen

We live in a time of confusion. So many young people are frustrated that some even take their own lives in despair. Thousands drop out of school, thoroughly discouraged, and others become part of the flotsam of society.

The suicide rate among teenagers is higher now than it has ever been, and has doubled in the last eight years. Significantly, it is highest among school dropouts and lowest among active students in school. The vast majority of today's youth, however, are stable and sensible, and are seriously planning to make a success of their lives.

Although today's youth is sometimes referred to as the "restless generation", the reference is limited to the noisy minority. The majority of our youth has no sympathy with the rioters, dissenters, or draft card burners. For the most part, they are well oriented and desire to work out their careers through honest effort.

A study was made recently on a national basis to determine what worries our teenagers most under today's conditions. The answers added up like this:

57 per cent worry most about getting well integrated into the established structure of the nation, succeeding in school and choosing a proper vocation.

29 per cent worried most about girls and their standing with their friends.

29 per cent listed family problems and the draft.

When the study asked what would please them most in life a significant 58 per cent said: "assuming useful responsibility." Only 12 per cent listed membership in "the gang" as most desirable and 13 per cent put down skill in sports.

Young people need not be thrown off balance by supposing that the majority of the youth of today is rebelling against the "establishment," burning down schools and banks which they did not build, and bombing government offices and business houses which they could not possibly replace. It is not the case. Most of them want to be in school. They want to learn profitable vocations, and hope to fulfill a useful purpose in life.

The national surveys show that gang life is ebbing and student rioting is declining. Significantly, most of our young people begin to identify the leaders of riots and dissention as agents of subversive groups, and are backing away from them. Personal achievement has continued to be the most persuasive element in their lives.

When the above-mentioned survey asked if they preferred to follow the heroes of their own generation or responsible adults, 94 per cent voted in favor of adult leadership. It was interesting also to note that sixteen-year-old boys said that of all adults they admire their parents most, and that they admire good character and vocational achievement more than any other quality in their adult acquaintances. Only 10 per cent considered glamour and appearance as of prime importance.

Latter-day Saint youths are most concerned about themselves, of course, and this is as it should be. And the youth of the Church today are wonderful! They are in a class by themselves in upholding clean and high ideals, and in their outlook upon life.

Since we are the children of God, our attitude toward him should should be most significant, and it is. Statistics show that 75 per cent of all boys in the Church are active in their wards or stakes. 52 per cent of all boys in the Church from twelve to nineteen are in priesthood meeting every week, reasonable excuses accounting for the remainder of the 75 per cent.

Of the girls of the same age, 65 per cent of them are in M.I.A. every week, with approximately 80 per cent of the total age group being active in the Church.

"Shall the youth of Zion falter" then? The answer is as decisive as the words of the hymn. "No! True to the faith!"

Further evidence is found in their response to the gospel, as is measured in their temple marriages. Ninety-five per cent of all graduates of our institutes of religion marry in the temple. Ninety-five per cent of B.Y.U. students marry in the temple.

In a study made over a ten-year period, and allowing time for them to subsequently marry, it was discovered that 87 per cent of the graduates of our seminary system married in the temple. In a study conducted among 18 stakes in the Los Angeles area, plus 22 stakes in the intermountain area and Northwest, it was discovered that 94.6 per cent of institute graduates there married in the temple, and of those who took some institute work but did not graduate, 83 per cent married in the temple.

To show the value of seminary and institute work in this regard, and the importance of attending, it was discovered in the study that among those students who took no seminary or institute work, only 19.6 per cent married in the temple.

Seminary and institute work is becoming more and more popular among the youth of the Church, assisting them to gain their life objectives. In 1955 there were only 37,284 students enrolled in seminary. By 1971 the figure had passed 120,000. In 1955 there were only 5,013 college students in our Church institutes of religion. By 1971 the figure approached the 50,000 mark.

It is of more than passing interest too that 59.3 per cent of all high school students who belong to the Church hold positions in their wards and stakes, showing their love for activity in religion, while 66.5 per cent of our institute students in college hold such positions.

Shall the youth of Zion falter? Directly the opposite. They are more active in the Church today than at any other time in our history, and there are more individuals now active than ever before.

We have more missionaries in the field than previously in more parts of the world, speaking a greater variety of languages, and receiving a broader knowledge of the cultures of various lands. We have an average of approximately 14,000 young people in the field constantly.

Are our young people happy in their religious life? They bear strong and enthusiastic testimony in the affirmative. They say over and over again that this is the life they love, and they LIVE — IT — UP!

Does It Help or Hurt?

Chapter Twenty

Do Church membership and activity help or hurt you in your search for a career? What does the world think about hiring "Mormons" in various business and professional fields? Do important firms want them or shun them?

The answer is readily found in the number of important companies which send representatives to the Brigham Young University to interview graduating students for employment.

Universally these interviewers say that BYU graduates are highly desirable, and that they are glad to have young people of the stability and character found among members of the Church. Some of our youth have mistakenly supposed that they could be hurt in their careers if they admitted they were "Mormons," but men who have remained faithful to the Church have found only respect on the part of their employers and most fellow employees.

What does the record show concerning the achievement of Latter-day Saints in public life, both industrial and professional?

Four Latter-day Saints have served recently in the cabinet of presidents of the United States, and were well known as Mormons among their associates. A "Mormon" woman served as treasurer of the United States during the Eisenhower administration.

A high priest in the Church served as judge of the U.S. Customs Court in the Port of New York. Another was U.S. ambassador to Mexico, later being released to become a member of the First Presidency.

A Latter-day Saint served as chairman of the U.S. Federal Reserve Board, another as chairman of the U.S. Tariff Comission, another as chairman of the powerful Federal Communications Commission, which controls the destiny of all radio and television stations in the nation.

A high priest in the Church served as administrator of the Federal Housing Administration in the United States, and still another, a Canadian, was minister of Land and Mines for that nation, and director of the Toronto Dominion Bank. An apostle of the Church served as world president of Rotary International, and was so introduced abroad.

Another active member was world president of Lions International, another leader of the American Medical Association, another was president of the National Manufacturers Association, one more is vice president of the American Cancer Society, while still another presided over the U.S. Junior Chamber of Commerce.

In the military we have had several generals who were faithful members of the Church. We have two rear admirals in the U.S. Navy.

Members of the Church have headed some of the nation's largest business firms, such as Woolworth's, the National Biscuit Company, grocery chains, banks, and insurance companies.

Others have excelled in science, education, and invention. A "Mormon" elder invented television, a high priest in the Church invented stereophonic sound, another was a close associate of Albert Einstein, another headed the U.S. space program.

At one time six large U.S. universities had active members of the Church as presidents. A "Mormon" high priest, a professor in the Harvard Graduate School of Business, became a widely accepted consultant for American business. A "Mormon" artist painted many of the scenes for Cecil B. DeMille's spectacular "The Ten Commandments." "Mormon" musicians and sculptors have received world acclaim.

Our Tabernacle Choir is heard over hundreds of radio and TV stations each week in many parts of the free world. Three "Mormon" women have been recent "U.S. Mothers of the Year."

Mormon girls have been Miss USA and Miss America, and a "Mormon" was recently declared America's Prettiest Girl. Another was acclaimed the National Teenage Girl of the Year. In the same year a "Mormon" boy from Hawaii was made National Teenage Boy.

Two Mormon families have won awards as the "All American Family." Mormon entertainers still hold the spotlight in some of the nation's best TV shows. "Mormon" athletes have won all "America's Most Valuable Player" awards, and championship trophies.

Does Mormonism help or hurt you? Mormonism is now accepted as a badge of merit and integrity. It can only reflect honor upon you.

What the "Big Ones" Say

Chapter Twenty-One

What do the great men of the world say about the importance of religion in achieving successful careers? What do they say about the validity of sincere faith in God?

Among the great success stories are those of the men who built great fortunes in America, and whose industries still dominate the economic world. Some of our industrial giants attribute their success to the payment of tithing to their various denominations. For example, Kenneth S. Keyes of the Keyes Foundation of Miami, Florida, writes:

"That tithing does pay financially as well as spiritually has been the experience and the testimony of many of our country's great business and financial leaders.

"William Colgate, of the great toothpaste and toilet preparation firm, was a tithe payer. Heinz, of 57 Varieties, Hershey of Hershey's Chocolate, Kraft of Kraft Cheese, Jarman, the shoe manufacturer, Hyde of Mentholatum, Kellogg of corn flake fame, Crowell of Quaker Oats, Kerr of Kerr Fruit Jars, Proctor, of Proctor and Gamble (Ivory Soap), Wannamaker, the department store king, are just a few of the well-known business leaders who honored God with their tithes and offerings.

"One time John D. Rockefeller Sr. was asked if he tithed. He replied:

'Yes, I tithe. My first wages amounted to $1.50 a week. The first week I took the $1.50 home to my mother, and she held the money in her lap and explained to me that she would be happy if I would give a tenth of it to the Lord.

'I did, and from that week to this day (this was said when he was an old man) I have tithed every dollar that God has entrusted to me, and I want to say to you that if I had not tithed the first dollar I made, I would not have tithed the first million dollars I made. Train the children to tithe and they will grow up to be faithful stewards of the Lord.'"

During the last world war the great generals of the allied armies were devout, prayerful men. Lord Montgomery, noted British general, was among the most outstanding in this respect, and made sacred worship a daily part of his routine. General Eisenhower, who later became president of the United States, did likewise, and when he was president, he repeatedly urged religious observance upon the citizenry.

Roger W. Babson, one of the great economists of the United States of a generation ago, published a book entitled: "The Fundamentals of Prosperity." In it he wrote this:

"Try as you will you cannot separate the factor of religion from economic development. In the work conducted by my organization at Wellesley Hills, Massachusetts, we study the trend of religious interest as closely as we do the condition of the banks, or of supply of and demand for commodities.

"Statistics of church membership form one of the best barometers of business conditions. Whenever the line of religious interest turns downward and reaches a low level, history shows that it is time to prepare for reaction and depression in business conditions. Every great panic we have ever had has been foreshadowed by a general decline in observance of religious principles.

"On the other hand, when the line of religious interest begins to climb, and the nation turns again to the simple mode of living laid by in the Bible, then it is time to make ready for a period of business prosperity.

"Reports received from all parts of the world show that the only development which can possibly keep democracy afloat is the revival of religion.

"Only religion can prevent democratic rule from developing into mob rule. A nation can prosper only as its citizens are religious, intelligent, capable of service and eager to render it. So the churches have the only solution to the problems of today.

"Most of the prosperity of this nation is due to the family prayers which were once daily held in the homes of our fathers. To a large extent, this custom has gone by. Whatever the arguments pro and con may be, the fact nevertheless remains that such family prayers nurtured and developed those spiritual resources to which the prosperity of the nation is due.

"The custom of family prayers should be revived along with many other good New England customs which some of the modern radicals may ridicule, but to which they owe all that they possess."

Men of science are often quoted and misquoted with respect to their attitude towards God and religion. It is refreshing to see what some of the greatest among them have to say.

Charles Darwin, who is held responsible for so much of the atheism in the world, largely due to a misunderstanding of the man, was in no sense even an agnostic. He was devout and a firm believer in the Almighty. Said he: "The question of whether there exists a Creator and Ruler of the Universe has been answered in the affirmative by some of the highest intellects that have ever existed." (p. 468, "The Descent of Man," Library Press, N.Y.C.)

Dr. Joseph W. Barker, former president and chairman of the Research Corporation of America and dean of the engineering school at Columbia University, in a commencement address at Ripon University, quoted in "Vital Speeches," explained that many scientists were misled by certain observations, and as a result came to conclusions which were atheistic.

"But now," he went on, "even the most pragmatic materialist, in the face of present day scientific knowledge, is led to the inevitable conclusion that the heavens declare the glory of God and the firmament showeth his handiwork."

His concluding remarks were: "As the children of Israel foreswore the worship of the golden calf and returned to the faith of Jehovah, so have we foresworn the crass mechanistic materialism and returned to that faith in God of which the Psalmist of old sang— 'the Earth is the Lord's and all that therein is.'"

Contrary to what many have supposed, Albert Einstein, one of the greatest scientists the world has produced, was a devout believer in God. He marveled at the universe and what it shows, and said: "The harmony of natural law reveals an Intelligence of such superiority that compared with it, all the scientific thinking and acting of human beings is an utterly insignificant reflection." (Pages 267-8, "The World As I See It")

At another time this great scholar spoke of the faith a scientist must have to do his work, and said, "I cannot conceive of a great scientist without this profound faith. Science without religion is lame, religion without science is blind." ("Einstein, Philosopher-Scientist," by Paul A. Schlipp.)

A Latter-day Saint scientist, Dr. Henry Eyring, was a close associate of Einstein, and reflected that scholar's views when he himself said:

"I am convinced that wise as men are, and in spite of the wonderful things they have done, the

Creator of the Universe goes so far beyond anything that men understand, that it is ridiculous to talk of the two in the same terms. So far as I have been able to observe, those who study deeply into scientific matters are often of that persuasion." ("The Faith of a Scientist," by Eyring.)

There are many others who might be quoted, such, for example, as Dr. Robert A. Millakin, California scientist, who said: "Nothing could be more antagonistic to the whole spirit of science than atheism. ... I think you will understand me when I say that I have never known a thinking man who did not believe in God." ("A Scientist Confesses His Faith"—Millakin.)

And when Dr. Arthur Compton, Nobel prize winner, wrote for "This Week" Magazine (Los Angeles Times), he said: "Few scientific men today defend the atheistic attitude. Design in the universe presumes an intelligence. Evidence points to a Beginner, a Creator of the universe. A physicist's studies lead him to believe this Creator to be an Intelligent Being."

And Sir Ambrose Flemming, British scientist, writing in his book, "The Origin of Mankind," said: "The ultimate cause of things and events is a self-conscious and personal living Being." Later on in his book he expresses his belief that the Creator is a person.

Professor Edwin Conklin, Princeton University biologist, writing in the Cincinnati-Times-Star, and repeated in the Reader's Digest, said:

"The probability of life originating from accident is comparable to the probability of the unabridged dictionary resulting from an explosion in a printing factory."

Writing in "The Evidence of God In an Expanding Universe," (G. P. Putnam's Sons, N.Y.C.) Dr.

Oscar Leo Brauer, physicist at San Jose State College, California, said: "Science can establish that a creative act at some time must have taken place, implying the existence of a divine Intelligence and a divine Power. Science can also establish that none but a divine Intelligence could have been the Author of the tremendous, involved, and intricate system of laws in the universe."

And Dr. Edward Luther Kessel, zoologist and professor of biology at the University of San Francisco, wrote: "To study science with an open mind will bring one to the necessity of a First Cause whom we call God. An open-minded scientist must heed the evidence and recognize that there must be a God."

But, of course, the greatest evidence for God comes through revelation, and we Latter-day Saints know that God lives because our modern prophets have seen him, and by the power of the Holy Ghost we have felt him and have come to know him.

You Only Live Once

Chapter Twenty-two

"If at first you don't succeed,
Try, try again."

That old adage applies to many things, but not to any second or third chance to pass through mortality. We only live once, so our efforts here had better be right. One significant step, sometimes seemingly very unimportant at first, can change the entire course of our lives.

Think back to Sue for a moment. Her date with Burt forced her to make a landmark decision. Two alternatives were suddenly and unexpectedly placed before her. She had no time to postpone it. There was no opportunity to deliberate in her mind. She had to decide immediately. There was Burt, making his advances. Should she fight or surrender? Burt wouldn't wait for her to weigh the consequences. What would she do? Her choices were these:

1 — She could give in to Burt and lose her virtue. If she were to choose this direction she would be labeled by the boys as an easy mark, a plaything to be toyed with and dropped, a girl of little character, and certainly not one that either Burt or any of his loose friends would marry.

She would have labeled herself in her own mind too, and for the rest of her life would never forget this one night in which a stain descended upon her purity, to be removed only through deep repentance, but even then, impossible to forget. She would have to be untrue to herself, her family, and to her God, for she was a Latter-day Saint who had been taught the law of chastity.

2— Her other choice was to drop Burt—popular as he was—and save her virtue. The temptation to be in the arms of the school idol indeed was great, but was she ready to pay the resultant price? When she saw Burt in his true light as an adulterous, pernicious, unchaste predator upon innocent girls, it wasn't so hard to make the decision. Seeing this side of him took away all the glamour. She saw in him only a low-living, filthy wretch, a robber of the worst kind, the kind who steals virtue, which should be held more dear than life itself.

One of the most important things about Sue's decision was that she realized that it held a significance for the remainder of her life, in fact, for all eternity. She was only living that hour of her life once. She couldn't erase a serious mistake and then try over again. Whatever she would do that night would become a part of the permanent record of her life. It would leave its mark indelibly upon her, for even after her repentance—if she had sinned—it would still live in her memory.

But is it not so with every decision we make— even the little ones? Are they not all significant? Do they not all merge to form our characters and our lives?

> Sow a thought, reap an act,
> Sow an act, reap a habit,
> Sow a habit, reap a life.

The Lord has given us a pattern for successful living. Elder Marion G. Romney once said about that pattern: "The Lord has not revealed to us a plan that will not work."

All of God's plans succeed. We will always prosper if we accept and follow them. That is why we have the gospel, which is the great overall plan. Jesus said it was given to us that we might have life, and have it more abundantly. That is what he offers us—the abundant life! If we accept it and live it consistently we shall have the desired result. But we must be consistent. We cannot be "hot" one day and "cold" the next, and expect to succeed.

We are both the architects and the builders of our lives. We may build of the good and durable materials which the Lord provides, or of the evil which Satan offers. But if we build with God, our house will rest upon a firm foundation, and when the winds blow, and the rains descend and the floods come, it will stand, because it is founded on a rock. But if we build on the shifting and uncertain sands of moral weakness, our house shall collapse and great shall be its fall.

We are the children of God. We are literally his offspring. We can become like him. That is our destiny. Shall we allow a moment's excitement to destroy that destiny? Shall we allow the allurements of popularity or prestige to interfere with it? Or shall be place our trust in God, and know that he will guide us successfully through life, and reward us eternally if we will but serve him?

One of our choice hymns pleads with the youth in these terms:

> "Cherish virtue, cherish virtue,
> God will bless the pure in heart.

And then it continues with:

"O prove faithful, O prove faithful,
To your God and Zion's cause."

So youth of the noble birthright, carry on, and Live It UP!

Index

A.

Abundant life, God offers us the, 105.
Adam and Eve placed first on earth, 48; and Eve married in holy union, 52.
Adult teachings, thankful for, 3; youth vote in favor of following, leaders, 90.
Adulterous relationship, trial marriage only an, 51.
Adultery, Lord speaks of sin of, 13; the Lord anciently made, a capital crime, 19; never a deterrent to divorce, 51.
Adults are as muddled as youth, hosts of, 19; wicked, will pay the price, 20.
Alma, Prophet, teaches chastity, 13.
America great, work made, 86.
"A New Significance," 81.
Atheism antagonistic to science, 101.

B.

Babson, Roger W., quoted on religious worship as a barometer of business, 98.
Baby racketeers, 20,000 girls fall into hands of, 18.
"Babylon," must not partake of the sins of, 7.
Baptism, Nicodemus told of importance of, 53.
Baptism font, sinful priests cannot please the Lord at the, 7.
Barbaric practices of today, 39.
Barker, Dr. Joseph W., quoted on scientists and religion, 100.
Beatles made "hot music" popular, 65.
Befool is to delude and deceive, 16.
"Better Homes and Gardens" poll on dating expectations, 6.
"Be ye clean that bear the vessels of the Lord," 8.

Bible a myth, many claim, 20.
Bodies are God-given, 7.
Body must pay for its stimulants, 83.
Born Free, 41; a poem, 45.
Boy's activity in Church is high 91.
Brauer, Dr. Oscar Leo, writes on "the creative act" and existence of a divine power, 102.
Brooke, Sen. Edward W., quoted on work, 88.
Brothels as in ancient Rome, we have same kind of, 39.
Brown, Bishop Victor L., speaks on basic differences of men and women, 69.
Burt and Susan on a date, 1.
B.Y.U. students marry in temple, 95 percent of, 91.

C.

Character, happiness anchored to good, 16; lying a vicious form of, assassination, 86.
Chastity, Savior taught complete, 13; Alma teaches law of, 13; each can steer into safe waters of, 21; only, will prevent venereal disease, 29; a safeguard for human act of reproduction, 48; Temple marriage based on complete, and virtue, 55; President David O. McKay speaks on dominant virtue of, 55.
"Cheapness, price tag of," 3.
Cheating in school a common form of dishonesty, 86.
"Cherish virtue," hymn quoted, 105.
Chicago has greatest incidence of venereal disease, 28.
Children have right to be well born, 48; parents should teach, in righteousness, 73; should honor parents, 74; commanded to honor parents, 76.

Christ is not divided, 59.
Church advice on steady dating, 31; 45 per cent of homes have no, affiliation, 60; leaders to train youth, 77; high percentage of, youth hold positions in wards and stakes, 92; membership and a career, 93.
Cigaret makers campaigned for women users, 62.
Civil marriage is man's mode, 55.
Clayton, Dr. James, quoted on low religious interest of youth, 60.
Clean, joy comes from the good and, 16.
Commandments, should obey Lord's, 59.
Common sense can restore healthful living, only, 66.
Compton, Dr. Arthur, writes on evidence of a creator, 101.
Conflict between human nature and divine nature, 38.
Conformance with law only way to progress, 43.
Confusion, live in a time of, 89.
Conklin, Prof. Edwin, quoted on origin of life, 101.
Consistency important in successful living, 105.
Corianton, Alma counsels son, 38.
Courtship cannot be a substitute for marriage, 33.
Creation, striking uniformity of all, 36.
Creative process, sex part of, 47.

D.

Darwin, Charles, a devout believer in the Almighty, 99.
Date, It's a, 1; a most important crossroad in life, 2; a, and long cherished aims, 2; how far to go on a,? 2; no, is worth a loss of virtue, 8; it is natural to, 31; "Whom Shall We,"?, 57; with plans for temple marriage, 60.
Dates among Latter-day Saint young people must never be for seductive purposes, 8.
Dating expectations of students, Howard Whitman conducts poll on, 6; the purpose of, 31; what about steady, 31; early, a mistake, 31; Church advice on, 31; people not of our faith, 60.
Death penalty decreed anciently for transgressors of law of chastity, 48.
Deceit and scheming a part of same package, 85.
Decisions we make, eternal significance of all, 104.
Degrading, petting is, 7.
Destiny to become like God, 47.
Devil, the Lord speaks of the, 85; "The, is a Liar," 85.
Devil's trap, sex abuse is the, 14.
Discipline, no training without, 76; progress and freedom only in self-imposed, 43.
Dishonest dealing an apostasy from Christianity, 88.
Dishonesty a part of modern way of life, 85.
Divine nature, conflict between human nature and, 38.
Divine purpose of sex, 47.
Divorce, adultry and fornication prime causes of, 51; a crushing burden, 17; Savior speaks of, 52; often results from mixed marriages, 59.
"Does It Help or Hurt?", 93.
Drug invasion, next came the, 66; long hair associated with, abuse, 67; the "thrill" element in the, habit, 82; use a vicious circle, 82.
Drugs becoming a frightful part of some dating habits, 18; experience of girl with, 18; hundreds killed by, 66; side-effects of, 66; leaders advise against habit forming, 81; use of, by students, 82; many youth misled to taking, 82; many youth die as victims of, 82.
Drunkenness is prevalent as ever, 39.

E.

Earth made as home for God's children, 47.

INDEX

Edison, Thomas A., quoted on work, 88.
Einstein, Albert, a devout believer in God, 100; quoted on faith of a scientist, 100.
Eisenhower, President, urged religious observance on citizenry 98.
Eternal beings, we are, 35; beings with an eternal destiny, 35; standards, 35; God and man are, 48; marriage is God's mode, 52.
Eternity, family relationship planned for, 52.
Evil, petting is, 6; association with, rubs off, 67.
Exaltation in eternity comes only to those married in Temple, 53.
Eyring, Dr. Henry, quoted on life in the universe, 36; quoted on power of Creator of Universe, 100.

F.

Fail, no one needs to, 16.
"Fair game" for boys, girls are not, 8.
Family relationship planned for eternity, 52; Lord taught greatest cohesiveness in, life, 74.
Father in Heaven, purpose of life is becoming like our, 16.
Femininity, women set aside their, 64.
Films, filthy, 23.
Filth, when restrictions are removed from, 20.
"Filthy Films," 23; experience of June Clark at a, 23-24.
Flemming, Sir Ambrose, expresses belief in a creator, 101.
Flight is best answer in some situations, 9.
Forgiveness possible for sex sin, 13; 49.
Fornication under same rule as adultry, 19.
Free agency to choose good or evil, man has, 38.
Free, born, 41; society is a self-disciplined one, 42.
Freedom of an individual to maintain right of privacy, 6; experience of girl who sought, 41; is being free to live under self-imposed law, 44.
Friends with plans for temple marriage, choose, 60.
Fun by itself is just a bubble, 16; is defined, 16.

G.

Galaxies, uniformity in all, 36.
Gambling is always bad, 66.
Gang life is ebbing, 90.
Generals were devout and prayerful men, many great, 98.
"Generation Gap, The," 73; Lord never intended there be a, gap, 74; there need be no, gap, 79.
Girls as objects of fun, 5; bodies are sacred, 7; are not toys or "fair game," 8; are better off without dates with evil boys, 8; hurt more than boys in era of moral confusion, 18; of Church have high activity, 91.
God, we are children of, 11; we are all the offspring of, 37; if faithful we will become like, 37; whims of men do not alter laws of, 38; only one formula to become like, 40; we are literal offspring of, 47; our destiny to become like, 47; has body of flesh and bones, 47; conditions for becoming like, 48; human line of descent provides bodies for children of, 48; disciplines us to become like him, 79; destiny of man to become like, 105.
God-given, our bodies are, 7.
God-like, all men can become, 40.
God's standards cannot change, 35; formula same for all his children, 37; judgments always just, 54; all of, plans succeed, 105.
Gonorrhea cases fifty times greater than syphilis, 28;

strains resistant to penicillin, 29.
Good people in world, still millions of, 11.
Gospel has two divisions, 53.
Gould, Charles L., writes "The Positive Side," 12.

H.

Hair, came into picture, long, 65; what is immoral about long,? 66; men in Paul's day wore short, 67; by association long, is a symbol of the moral revolt, 67; Paul speaks of shame of long, on man, 70.
Happiness in sin, no, 13; definition of, 16; inchored to good character, 16; a result of righteous living, 68.
Hippie element adds new dimension in degradation, 65.
Hoffer, Prof. Frank W., quoted on "price tag" of cheapness, 3.
Holy Ghost is first great sin, sin against, 13; worst of all sins is that against, 49.
Homes, illicit sex acts have broken more hearts and, 52; plight of many youth traceable to inadequacy of, 73.
Homosexual activity given legal status, 19.
Homosexuality same as practiced anciently, 39; legalized by some legislatures, 65.
Homosexuals anciently executed, 19; among worst carriers of venereal disease, 28; about 20 million, in U.S., 28.
Honest effort, successful careers depend on, 86.
Honesty, a quotation of Pres. David O. McKay, 87.
Hoover, J. Edgar, quoted on "Shall I Force My Child," 75.
"Hot music" then came, 65.
Human nature should develop into divine nature, 38; has never changed, 39.
Human reproduction differs from other forms of life, 48.

I.

Idle mind is devil's workshop, 86.
Illegitimacy, new highs in, 17.
Immoral, new laws passed to protect the, 19.
Immorality paraded under guise of "a new morality," 19.
Indulgence is downward living, 15.
Insincerity a part of modern way of life, 85.
Institute graduates marry in temple, 95 percent of, 91.
Isaac, Abraham sought believing wife for, 58.

J.

Jacob, believing wife sought for, 58.
Jesus was the Firstborn of God, 47.
Joseph and Potipher's wife, moral law today is same as with, 38.
Joy as defined by Webster, 16; of growth is the deeper emotion, 16.
Judgments are always just, God's, 54.

K.

Kessel, Dr. Edward Luther, writes on there must be a God, 102.
Keyes, Kenneth S., writes on prominent tithepayers, 97.
Knowledge increasing, man's reservoir of, 38; folly to spurn, 77.

L.

Ladder should be our choice, not the toboggan, 16.
Latter-day Saint boy should lead a girl into a moral trap, no, 9; no, girl should hesitate to run out on a date, 9; youth should be on the "Lord's side," 25.
Latter-day Saints must be different, 7; should marry Latter-day Saints, 57; faithful, respected by employers, 93; achieve-

ments of, in public life, 93; head some of nations largest business firms, 94; excell in science, education and invention, 95.
Law provides legal punishment for crime, 43; conformance to, puts man on moon, 44.
Laws provide freedom and protection for majority, 42.
Liar, scriptures teach the devil is a, 85.
Liberation and standards, advocates of, 17.
Life, true purpose of, 16; scientists quoted on, on other planets, 36; conformance to law is the way of, 44; protect virtue above your, 49.
"Like Men or Like Women?", 69.
Linkletter's daughter trapped into drug situation, 82.
Liquor interests appealed to women, 63.
Live it up!, noble youth advised to, 106.
Lives, we are architects and builders of our, 105.
"Living it up," Burt talks of, 5.
"Living It Up—or Down," 15.
Lord condemns illicit sex relations, 13; allows no sex act outside of legal marriage, 51; commands parents teach their children, 77.
Los Angeles County, high rate of venereal disease in, 28.
Lucifer seeks to destroy fountains of life, 49.
Lustful, petting is, 7.
Lusting after woman, rule given on, 14.
Lying as despicable as stealing, 85.

M.

Magazines, filth invades, 20.
Male students dating expectations, 6.
Man should be masculine, scriptures emphasize, 71.
Marriage, pairing off in honorable, 31; courtship can never be a substitute for, 33; provides for children to be born with blessing of God, 48; and chastity safeguards for human act of reproduction, 48; can neither be a trial or experiment, 51; intended to be permanent, 51; world today loses sight of true meaning of, 52; God's mode of, is eternal, 52; in temple is important, 54; Lord counsels against, with unbelievers, 58.
Marriages, No Trial, 51; problems facing mixed, 58.
McKay, Pres. David O., quoted on happiness and rearing families, 55; quoted on "Honesty," 87.
Men adjusted estimate of women, 64.
Millakin, Dr. Robert A., quoted on atheism as antagonistic to science, 101.
Mini-skirt was born, 64; sex crimes rocketed with advent of, 64.
Missionaries of Church increase to 14,000, 92.
Mixed marriages, problems of, 58.
Moon, rocks similar to those of earth, 36; natural laws governing the, 43; conformance to law puts man on, 44.
Moral breakdown from Second World War, 5; collapse follows removal of restrictions, 19; laws of God do not change, 38; revolution followed World War II, 61; long hair a symbol of, revolt, 67.
Morality cult, petting one of traps of the new, 6.
Morals, should be concerned about good, 11; pornography promotes destruction of, and good character, 24.
Mormon athletes have excelled, 95; entertainers on some of best T.V. shows, 95; many, women have had national recognition, 95.
Mormonism now accepted as a badge of merit, 95.

Movies lead youth into sex traps, suggestive, 24; fearlessly display carnal sex scenes, 65.
Moses' day, Lord speaks of divorce in, 52.
Muddled standards, 17; why are youth?, 19.
Murder is second greatest of sins, 13; no one has right to commit, 43; is second greatest sin, 49.

N.

Nature are eternal, God's formulae for, 35.
Nature's laws unchangeable, 43.
Newspapers, filth invades, 20.
Nicodemus told of importance of baptism, 53.
Night clubs began fad of "topless" and "bottomless" waitresses, 65.
"No Trial Marriages," 51.

O.

Occult is with us today, 39.
Ordinances necessary to exaltation, all, 53.

P.

Parenthood next to Godhood, 49.
Parents so with children, as with, 60; mistakes of, are perpetuated, 73; errant youth complain against, 73; should teach children in righteousness, 73; deliberately evil and cruel toward children, 74; should honor children, 74; most, are worthy of honor and gratitude, 74; commanded to teach children, 76.
Pattern for successful living, the Lord has given us a, 105.
Paul counsels: "Be not unequally yoked together, 58; said men in his day wore short hair, 67; speaks on appearance of men and women, 70; speaks of shame of long hair on man, 70; writes on obedience of children, 78.
Peale, Norman Vincent, quoted on dishonesty, 88.

Peculiar people, Latter-day Saints must be a, 7.
Penney, J. C., quoted on work, 88.
Pep pills take away vitality, 83.
Perfection, gospel is formula for, 37; no, in filth or moral deviation, 39.
Permissive, our age has become, 19.
Personal achievement still is most persuasive element in life of youth, 90.
Petting tendency growing among youth, 5; is evil, 6; one of traps of the "new morality cult," 6; no justification for, 6; is lustful, sensual, degrading, 7; cannot be without lust, 13; nothing virtuous in, 13.
Planets have same elements, 36; are other, inhabited?, 36.
Pill, dangerous "side-effects" of the, 20; the, removes lid of restraint, 20; and contraceptives promote promiscuity, 65.
Pornographic publications multiply, 20; books and magazines become best sellers, 65.
Pornography appeals to the baser nature, 24.
"Positive Side, The," by Charles L. Gould, 12.
Pre-marital sex approved by some as trial marriage, 19; nothing more than fornication, 51.
Priesthood powers, Latter-day Saint boys hold, 7.
Promiscuity costs, what, 27.
Prosperity defined, state of, 16.
Prostitution at 16, girls allowed to enter, 19; legalized for sixteen-year-olds, 65.
Psychiatric load, a greatly increased, 17.
Pure, God is, 39.
Purity of mind and body, Lord commands, 29.
"Purpose of Dating, The" 31.

R.

Rape increases 400 per cent in Tokyo, 64.

INDEX

Religion in family, should be a unity of, 58; mixed marriages often result in giving up all, 59; college students have little interest in, 60; great men speak on importance of, 97.

Religious unity, the Lord seeks to preserve, 59; Church youth happy in life, 92.

Repentance and obedience is always the escape, 20.

Revelation is greatest evidence for God, 102.

Righteous persons to receive all saving blessings, 53.

Righteousness, repentant will receive rewards of, 20.

Rioting of students is declining, 90.

Rock groups, long hair associated with, 67.

Rockefeller, John D., quoted on worth of man's word, 86; quoted on tithing, 98.

Rogers, Will, quoted on work, 88.

Romney, Elder Marion G., quoted on workability of the Lord's plan, 105.

Rotary International, apostle of Church served as president of, 94.

S.

Sacrament table, sinful priests cannot please the Lord at the, 7.

Safe than sorry, better be, 9.

Salt, formula for table, 36.

Sanctity of Sex, The, 47.

Satan drags sex into degradation, 47.

Savior and long hair, question of the, 67.

School, thousands drop out of, 89.

Selfishness cause of most generation conflicts, 74.

Seminary graduates marry in temple, 87 per cent of, 91; value shown of, and institute programs, 92; popularity of, and institute programs, 92.

Sensual, petting is, 7; films promote unchastity, 64; lyrics for songs, 65.

Sex sin one of three greatest in world, illicit, 13; Lord condemns illicit, relations, 13; Lord tells us to refrain from, sin even with our eyes, 14; abuse is the devil's trap, 14; costs of promiscuous, indulgence, 27; made a social football, 47; The Sanctity of, 47; is something sacred and pure, 47; part of creative process, 47; profaning the, act becomes one of worst sins, 47; Adam and Eve reproduced through pure, 48; is sacred to the Lord, 48; sins come next to murder, 49; sins may be forgiven, 49; Satan inspires demoralizing emphasis on, 49; crimes rocketed with advent of mini-skirt, 64; acts discussed openly, 64; no true Mormon boy or girl would knowingly become a symbol of the, revolt, 67.

"Sex appeal" gimmick, then came the, 64.

"Shall I Force My Child" by J. Edgar Hoover, 75.

Shapley, Dr. Harlow, writes on life on other planets, 36.

Short Skirts—Long Hair, 61.

Significance of all decisions we make, 104.

Sin is not desirable, 13; no happiness in, 13; no happiness in any kind of, 68.

Sinful priests cannot please the Lord, 7.

Slave to passions and appetites, being a, 42.

Slothful worker honorable, is the?, 86.

Smartt, Dr. Walter H. tells of syphilis increase in Los Angeles, 28.

Smith, Joseph, quoted on "no one can be saved in ignorance," 77.

Social groups, L.D.S. youth urged to form own, 8.

Sodom and Gomorrah, immorality always ends like, 20.

Solomon quoted on "train up a child," 78.
Spirit clothed in flesh, God is a, 48.
Standards, muddled, 17; of conduct are always the same, 40.
Steady dating, what about, 31.
Stimulants, Lord advises against artificial, 81.
Students quoted on going steady, 31.
Style, youth had to be in, 65.
Succeed, all God's plan, 105.
Success, God gave us guidelines to, 16.
Suicide, multiple increase in teenage, 17; rate among teenagers higher than ever, 89.
Susan, experience on a date with Burt, 1; faces grave decision, 2.
Sue's decision shows realization of significance for all eternity, 104.
Syphilis, tragic results of, 27; high cost of combatting, 28.

T.

Tabernacle Choir heard over hundreds of radio and TV stations, 95.
Teacher necessary to learning process, 79.
Television, Mormon Elder invented, 95.
Temple marriage is God's mode of marriage, 52; ordinances are saving ordinances, 53; Lord speaks of those who reject, marriage, 53; marriage is important, 54; marriage based on complete chastity and virtue, 55.
Temples of Holy Spirit, our bodies are, 7; some ordinances reserved for, 53.
Testing planned to prove our worthiness, 48.
Thrills, more to life than, 15.
Tithing, John D. Rockefeller quoted on, 98.
Toboggan, indulgence puts us on a, 15.
"Today's World," 89.

Toys, girls are not, 8.
Training opens door to skill and achievement, 76.
Trial marriage, pre-marital sex approved by some as, 19; urged periodically, 51; is literally pre-marital sex, 55.
Trial Marriages, No., 51.
T.V. Stations, filth invades, 20.

U.

Unbelievers, Lord cautions against involvement with, 8.
Universities, Mormons Presidents of six, 95.
U. S. space program, Mormon heads, 95.

V.

Venereal disease, 400 per cent increase in, 17; disease spread by promiscuity, 27; disease now an epidemic, 27; what of treatment of, disease, 28; no medical preventative for, disease, 29; only chastity will prevent, disease, 29; disease raised head with awesome results, 65.
Virtue, petting a partial loss of, 6; no date is worth a loss of, 8; maligned and ridiculed, 17; more important than preservation of life, 49.

W.

Water, formula for, 35.
"What the Big Ones Say," 97.
Whitman, Howard, reports on poll of dating expectations of students, 6; writes on greatest hurt to girls, 18; relates experiment on early dating, 31.
Wisdom of growing youth?, whence this, 73.
Woman should be feminine, scriptures emphasize, 71.
Women joined the military, 61; status of, changed, 62; began to demand rights, 62; induced to drink liquor, 63; down came standards of, 63.

Word of Wisdom a most important relevation, 81; should alert every Latter-day Saint against drug abuse, 81; today has a new and added significance, 83.
Work honorable if done honestly, 86; great leaders quoted on, 88; God commanded man to, 88.
Worthiness, testing planned to prove our, 48.

Y.

"You Only Live Once," 103.
Youth can find wholesome companionship in Church, 8; will pay the price for own sins, 20; "and the Natural Urge," written by Howard Whitman, 33; should make any sacrifice to obtain temple marriage, 54; should honor their elders, 77; majority of, are stable, 89; worries listed, 90; most of today's, want to be in school, 90; of Church today are wonderful, 91.

Z.

"Zion is the pure in heart," 9.